Adult Coloring Book

Stress Relieving Designs & Patterns

By Mastal

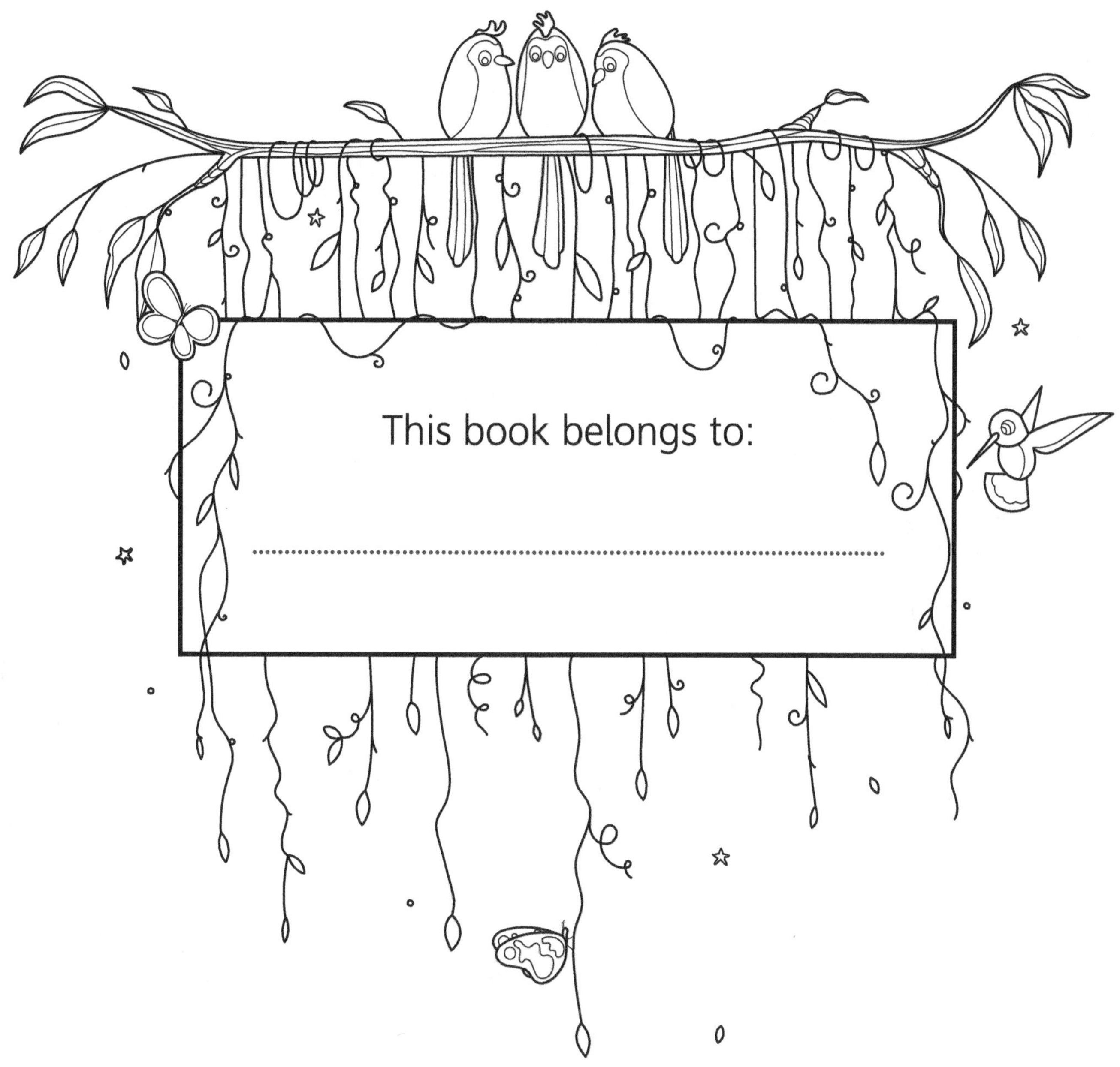

This book belongs to:

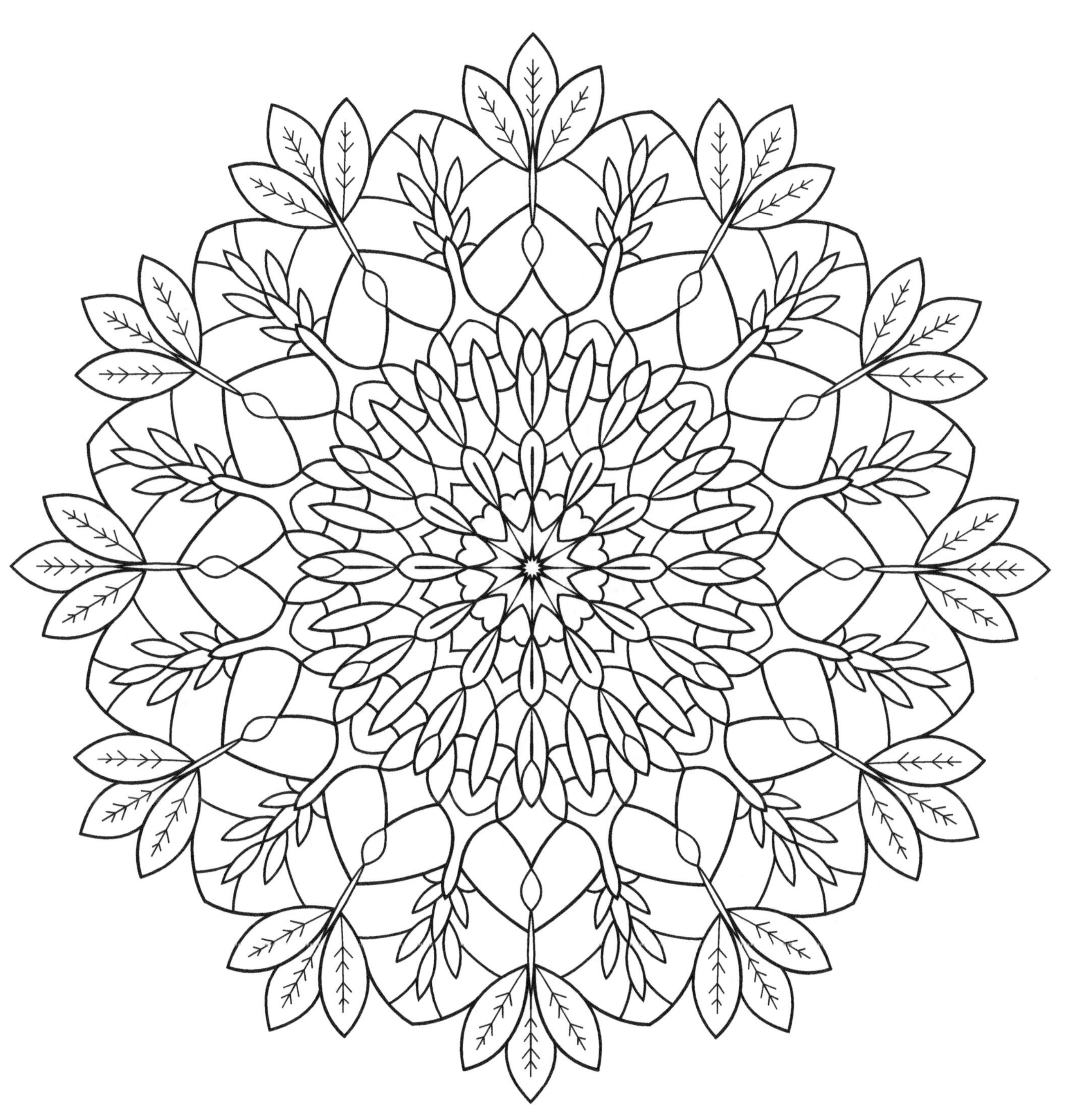

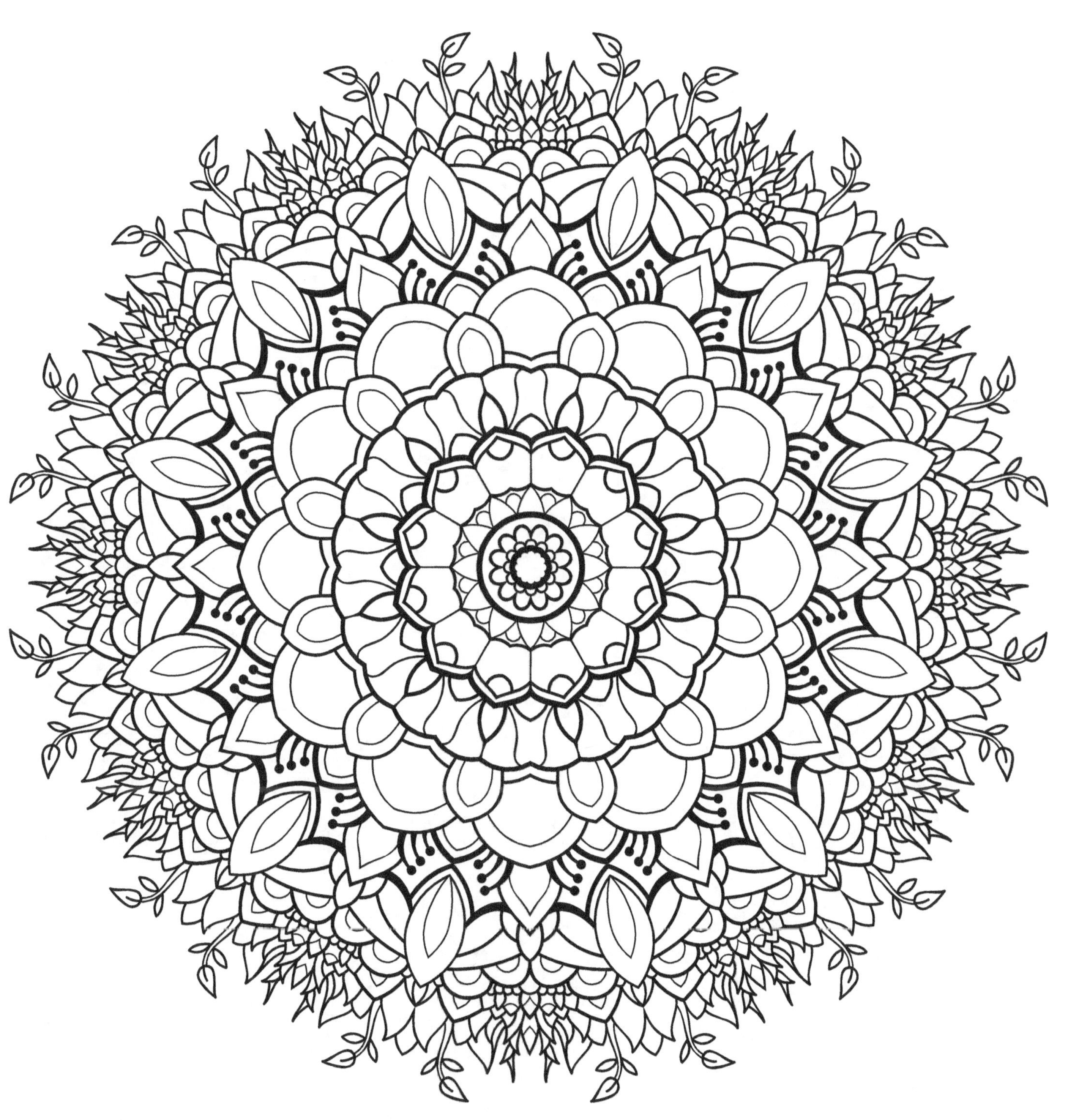

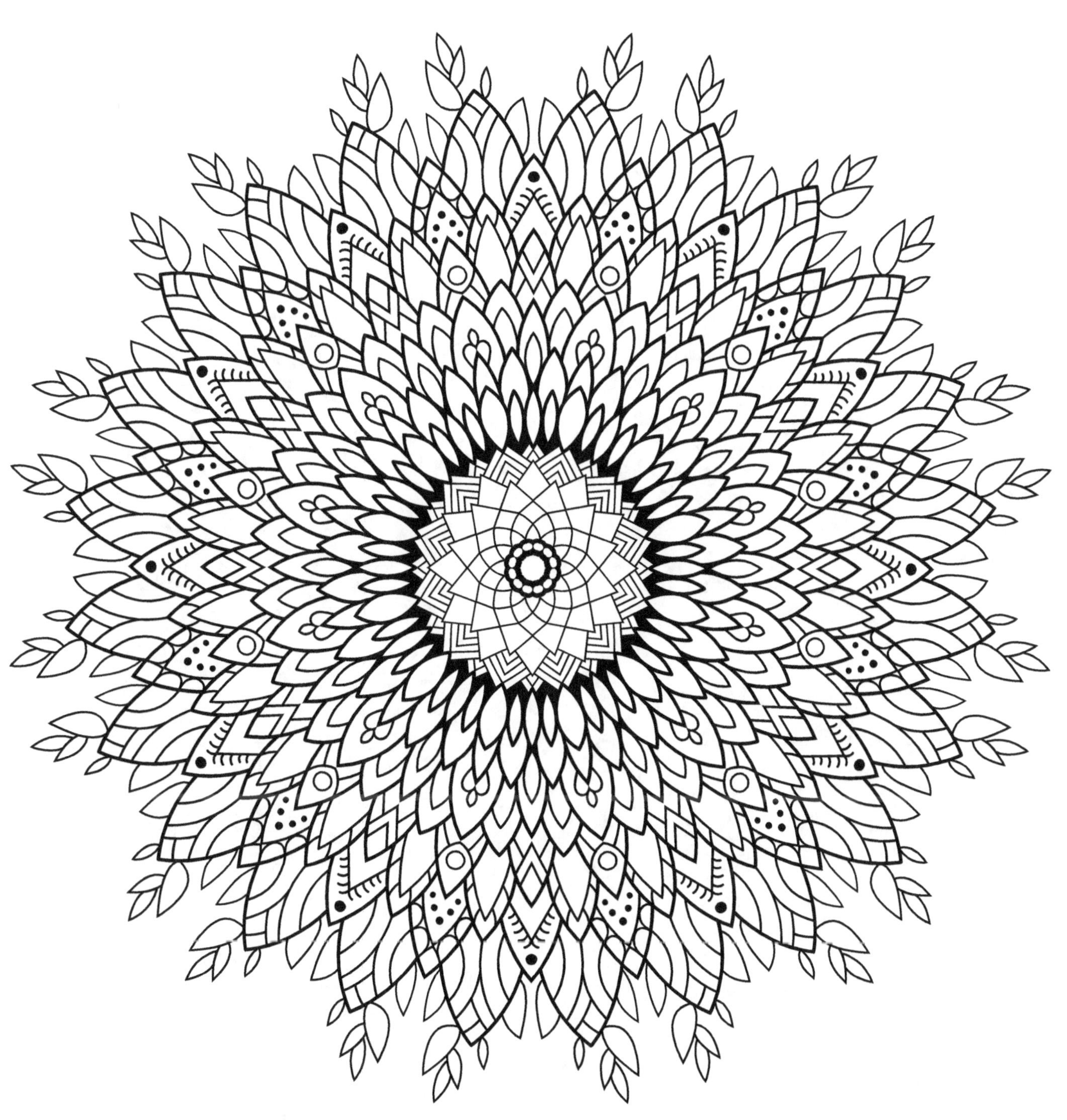

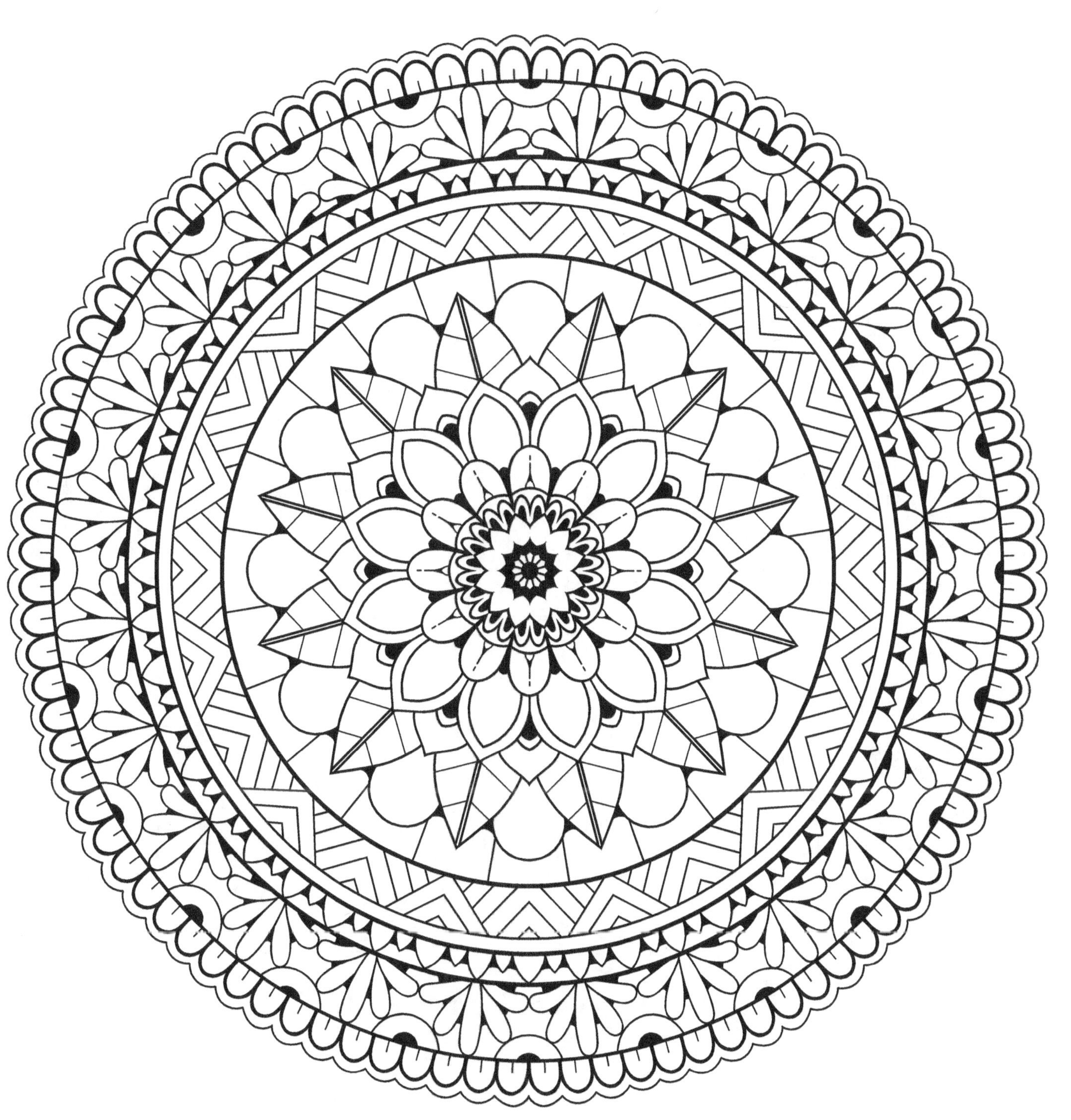

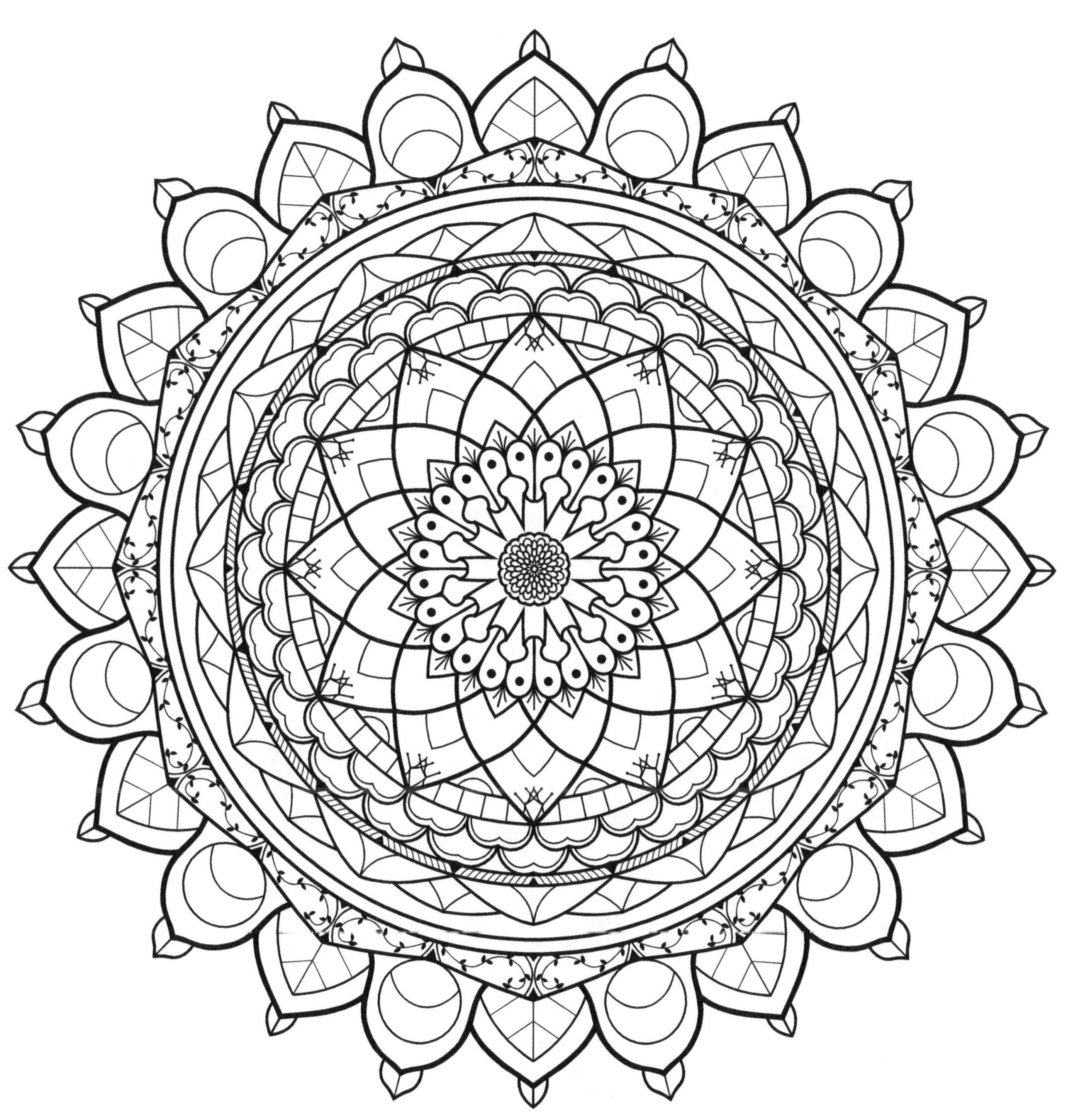

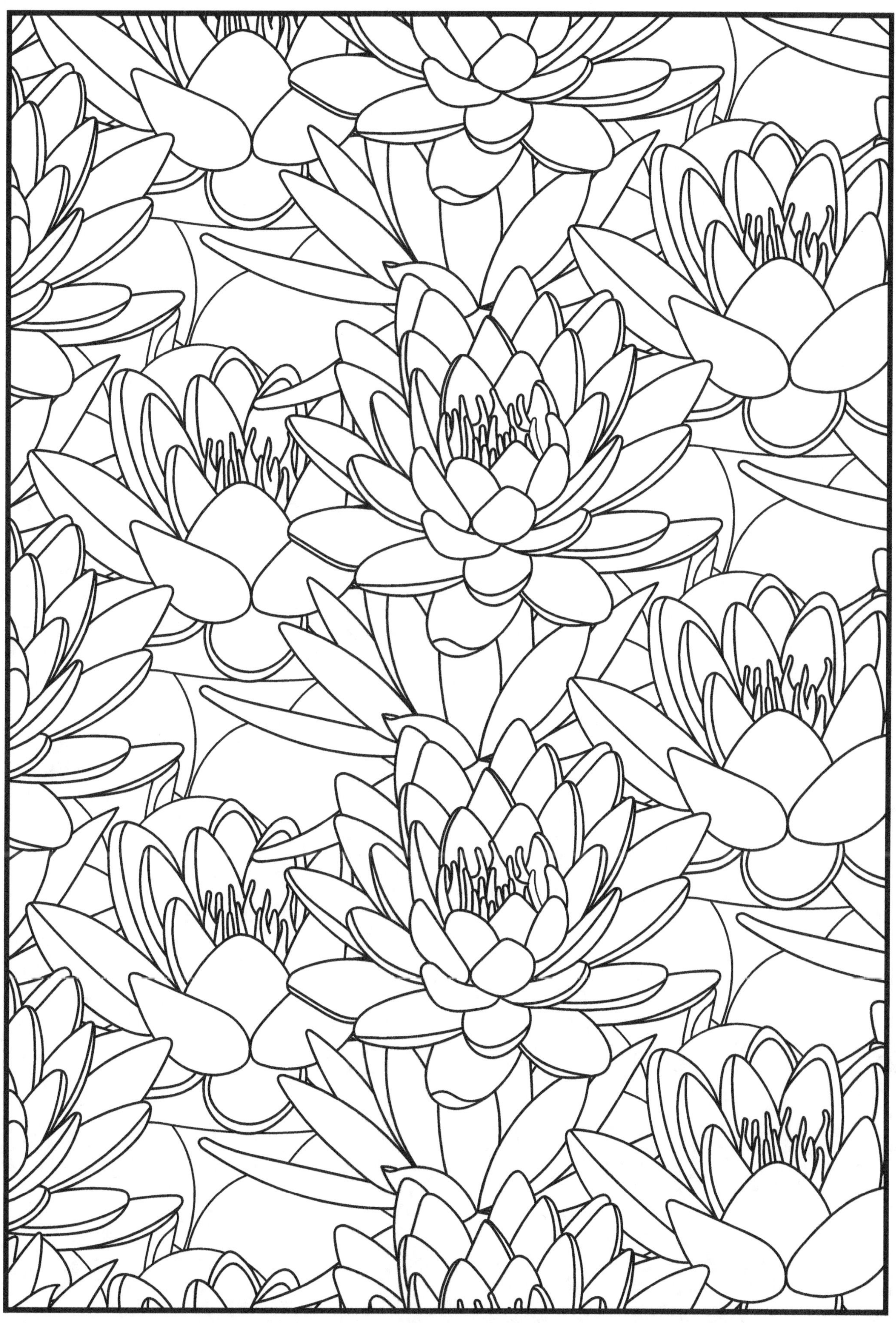

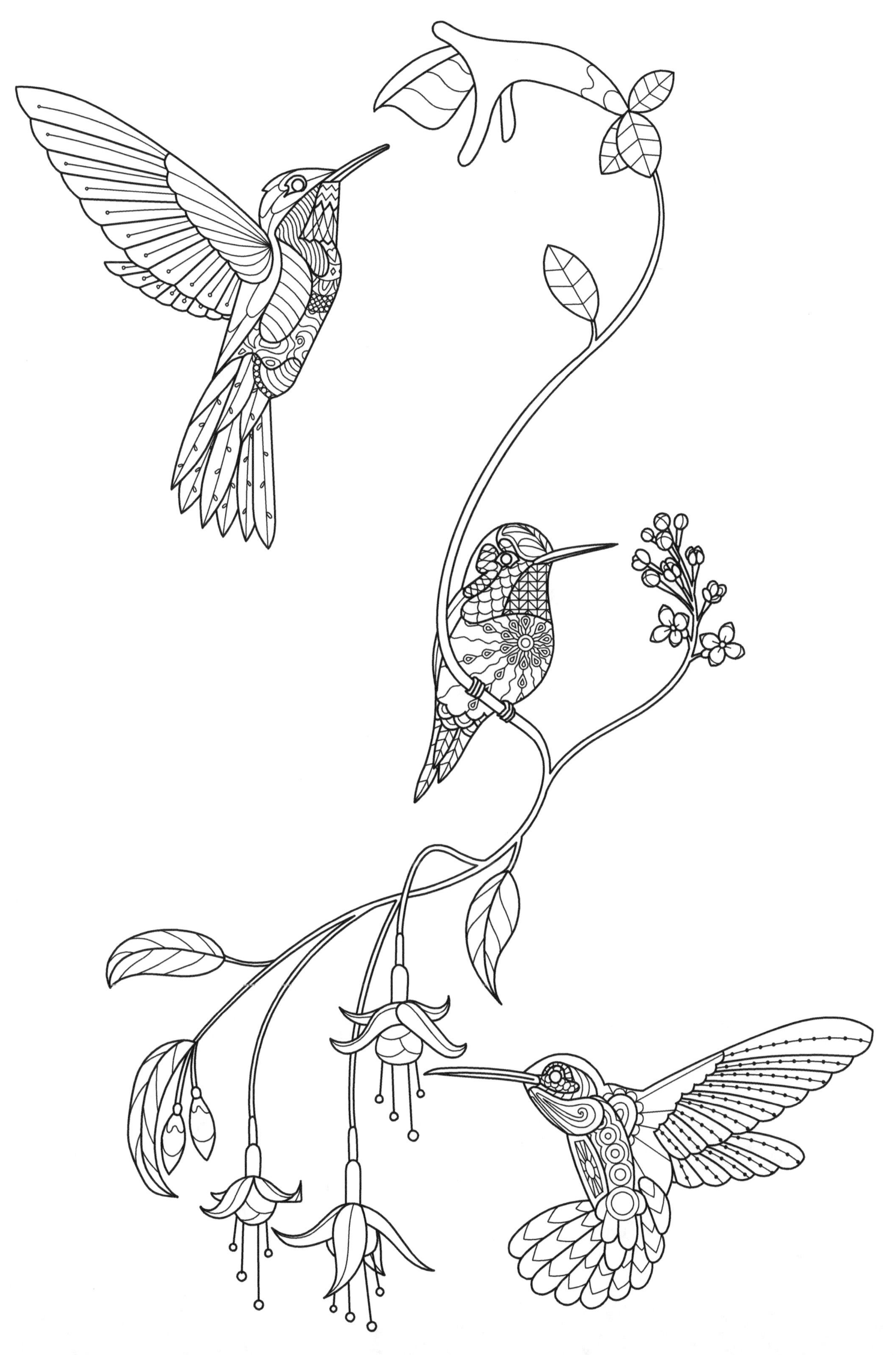

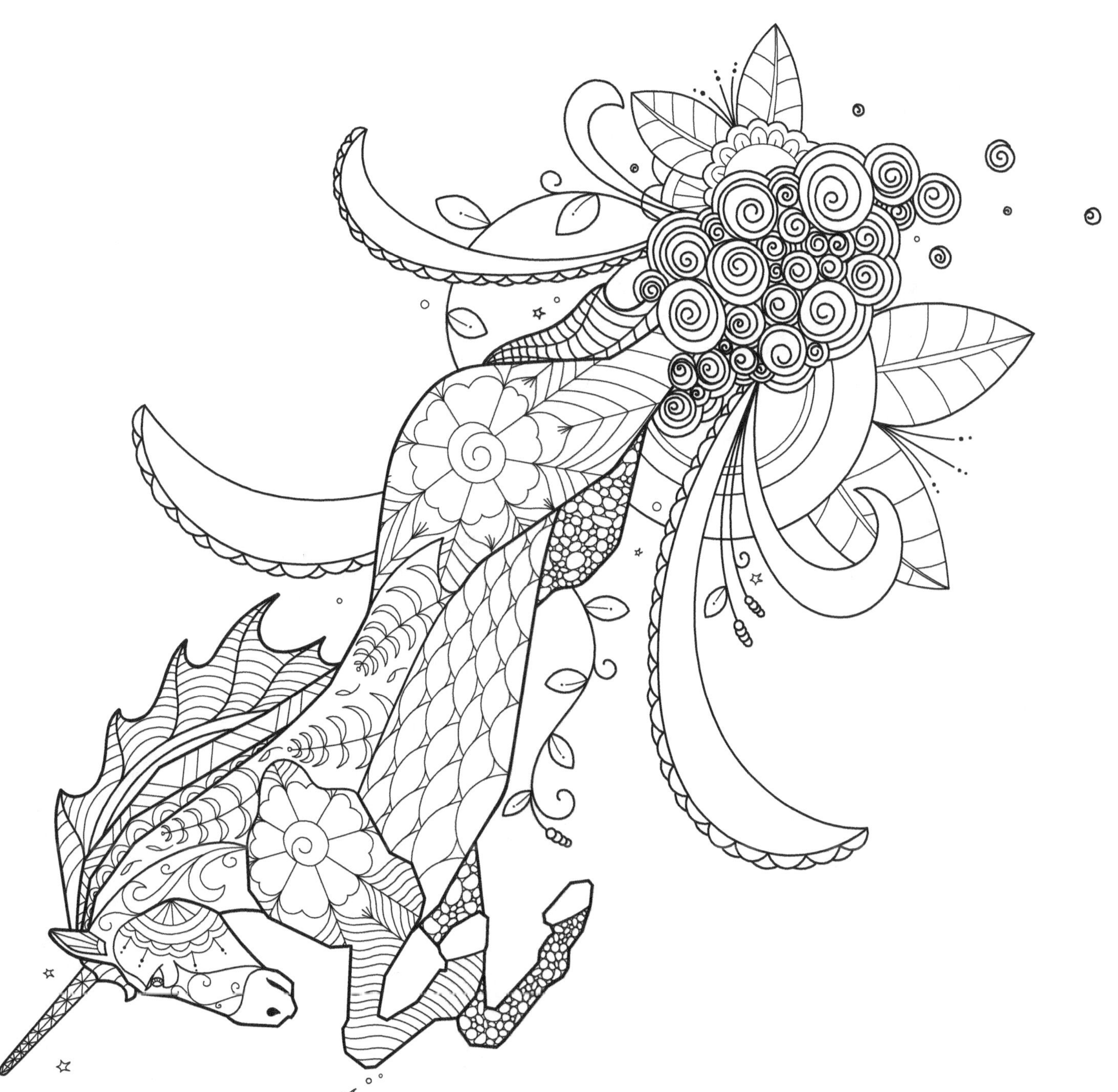

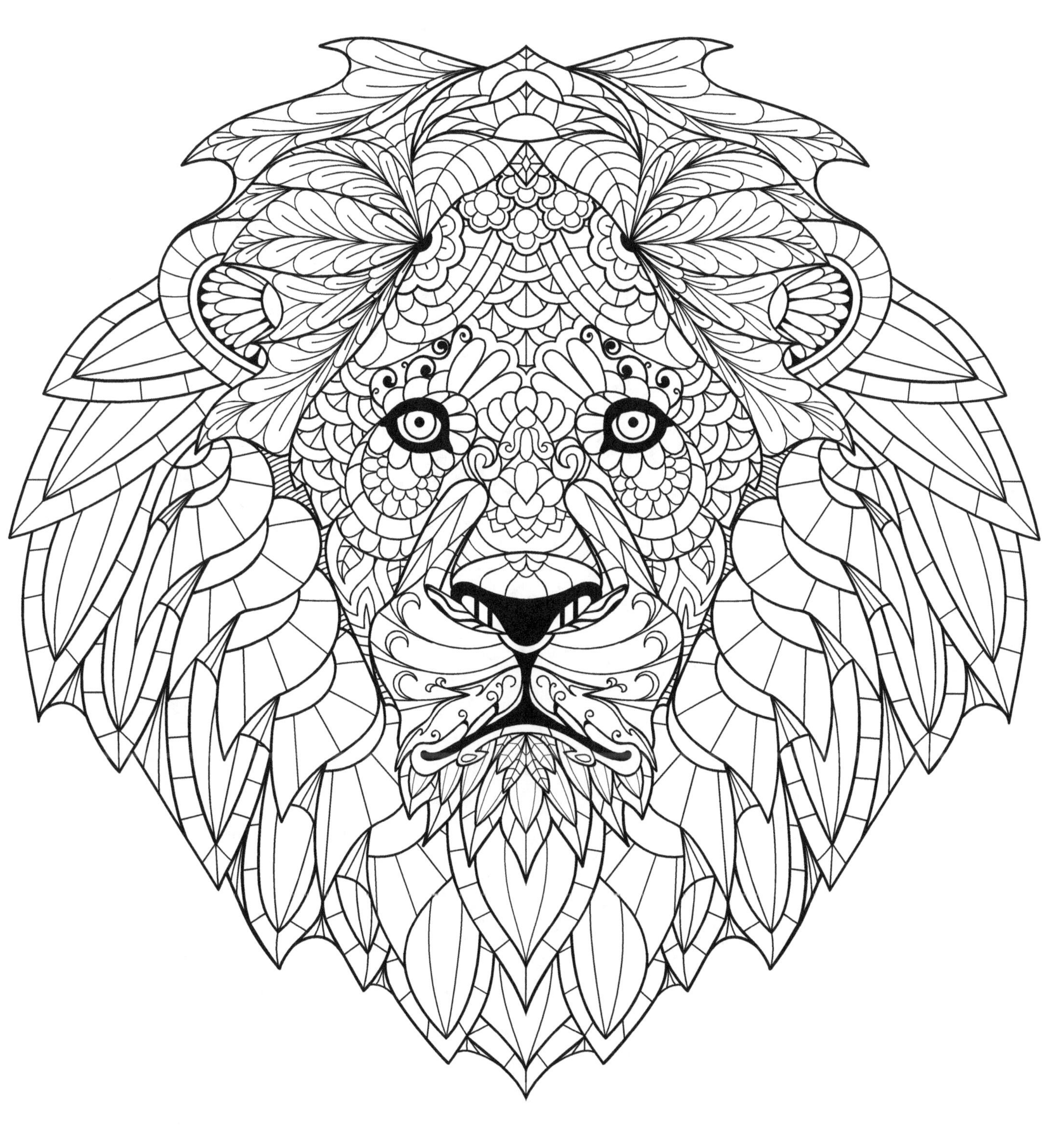

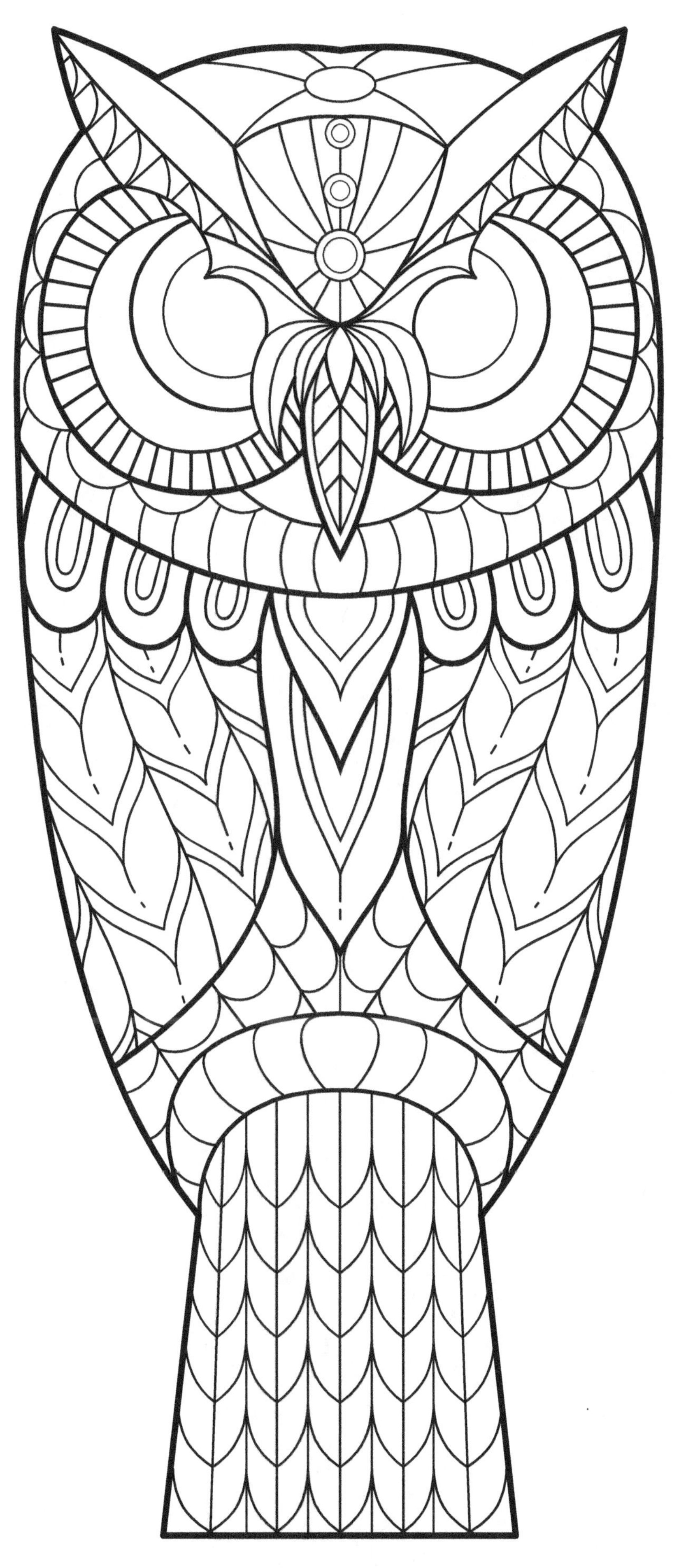

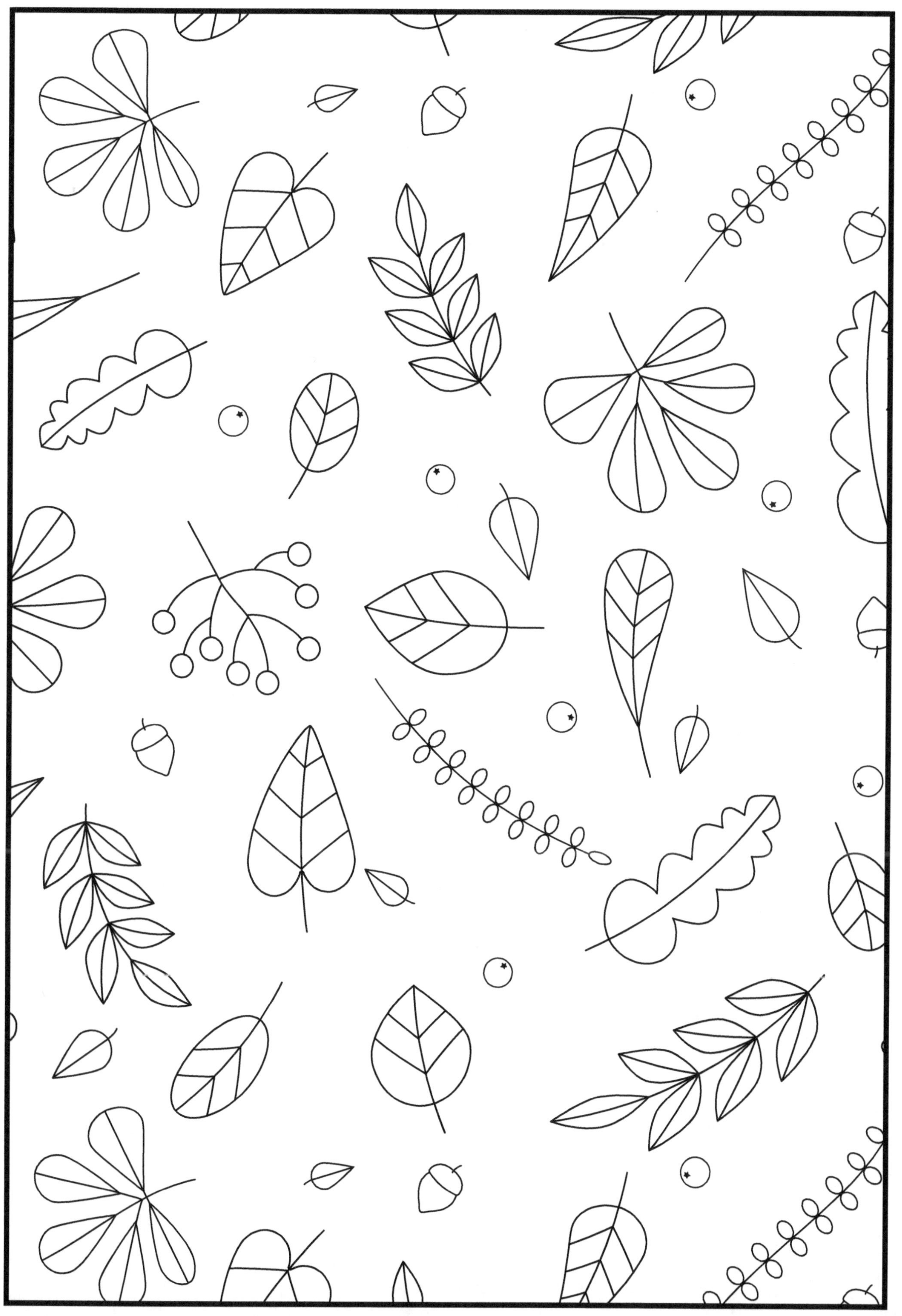

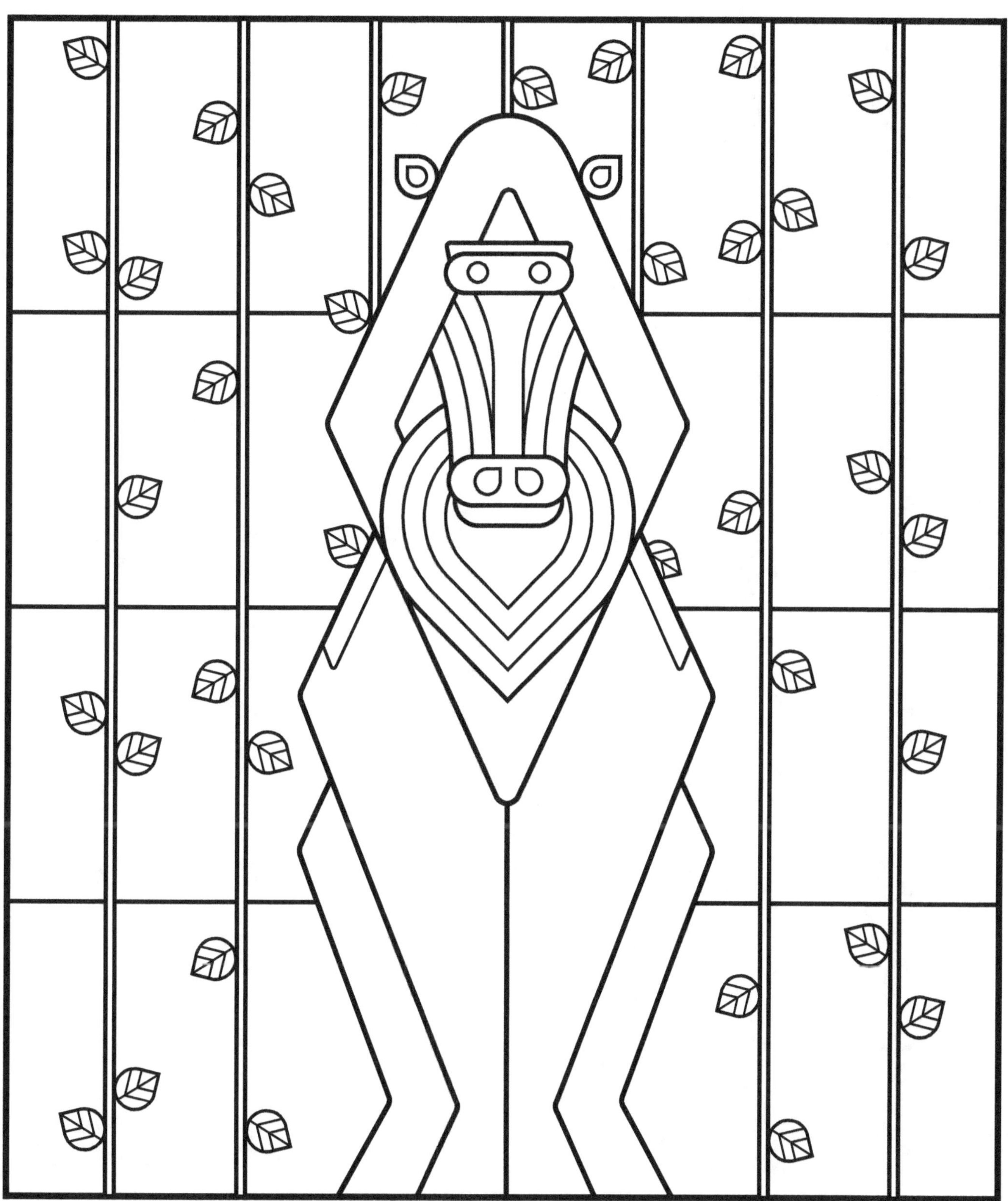

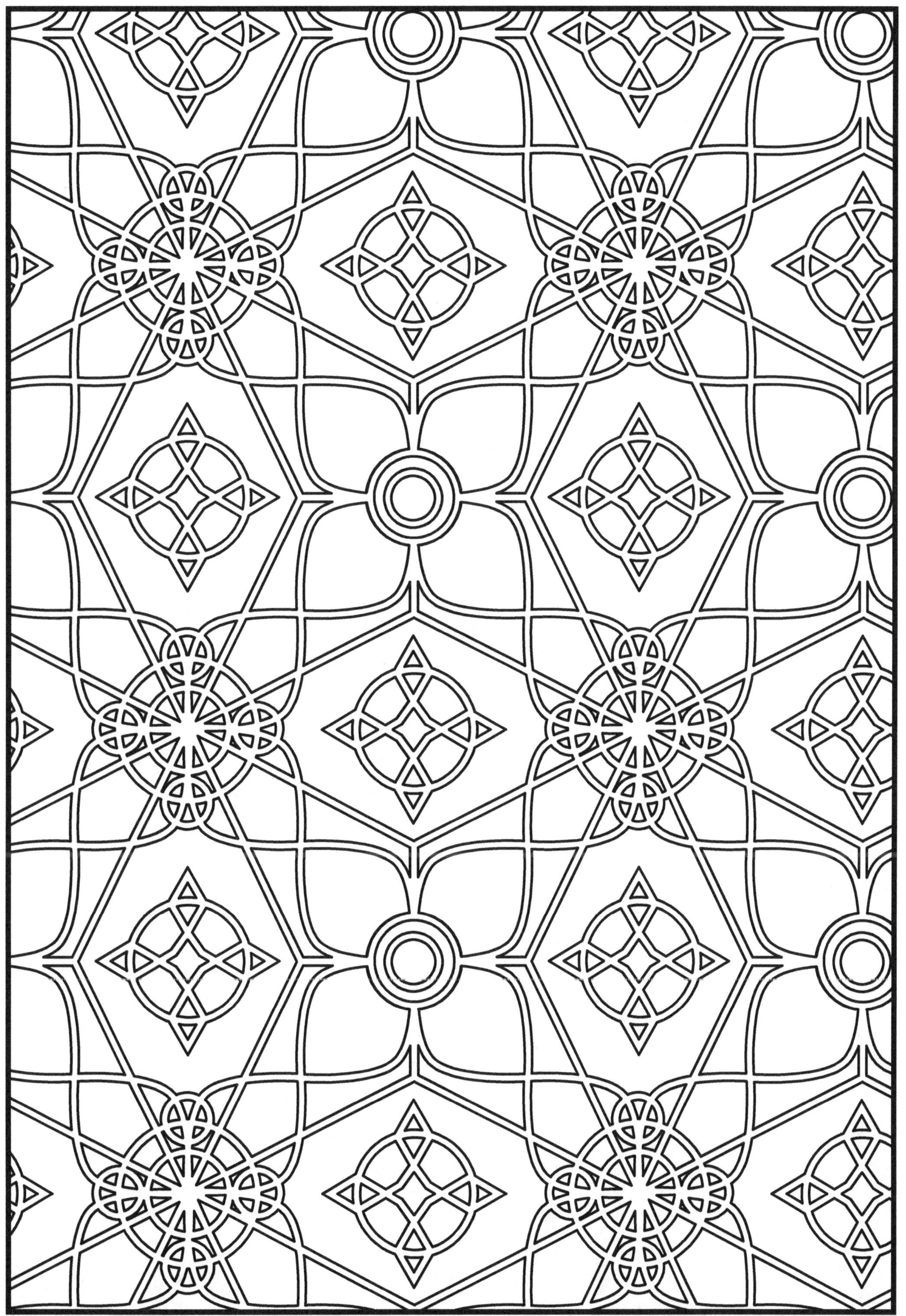

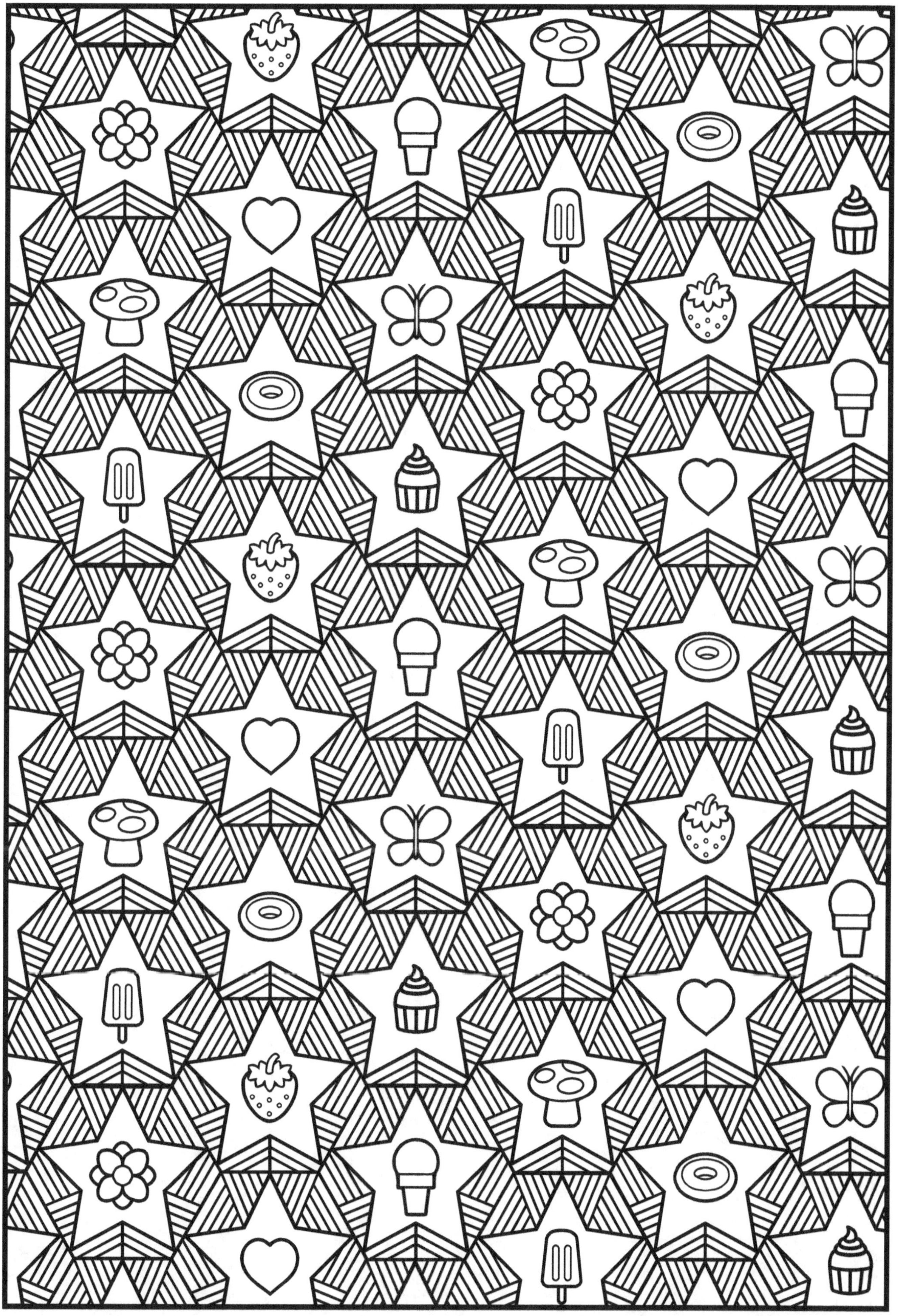

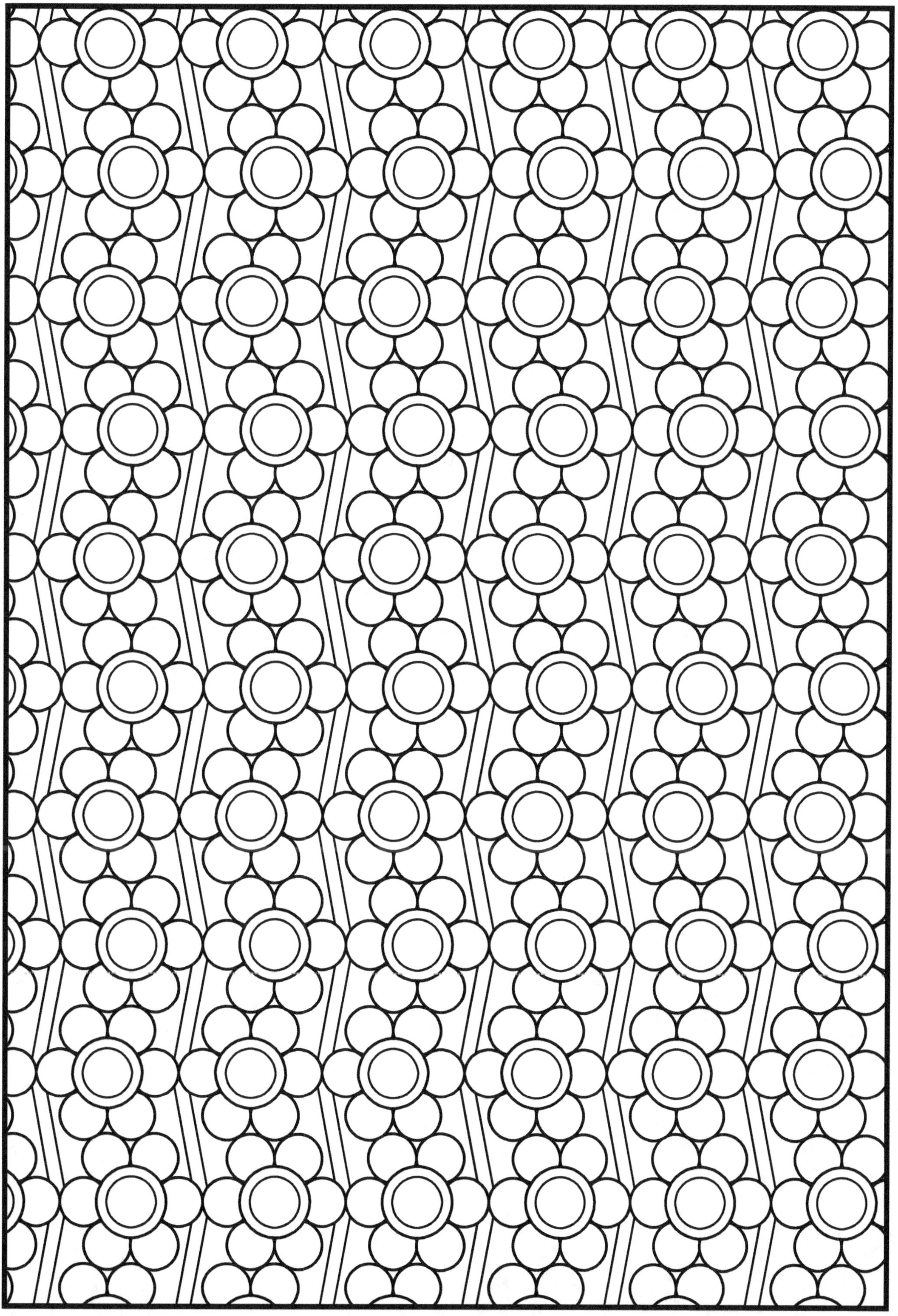

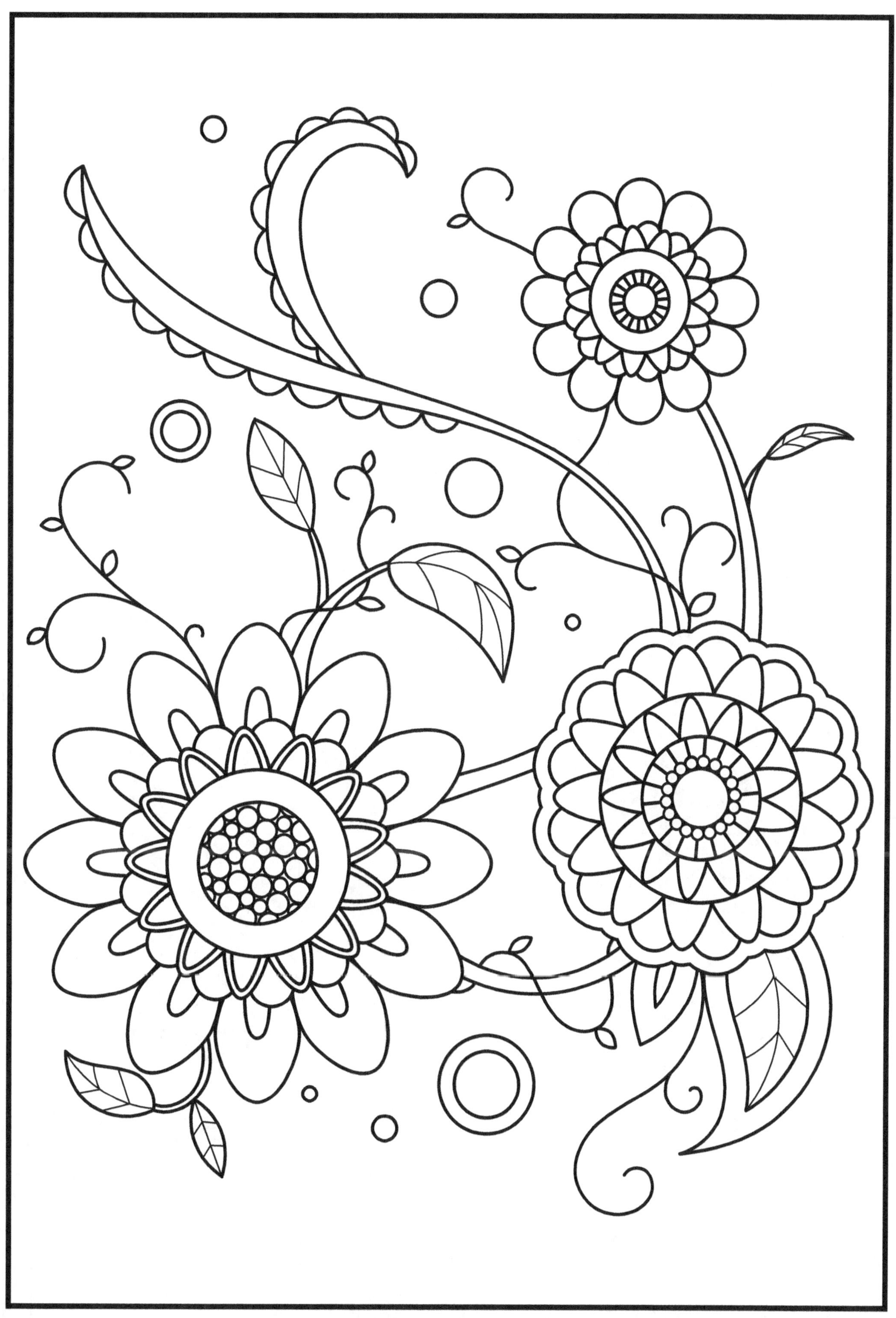

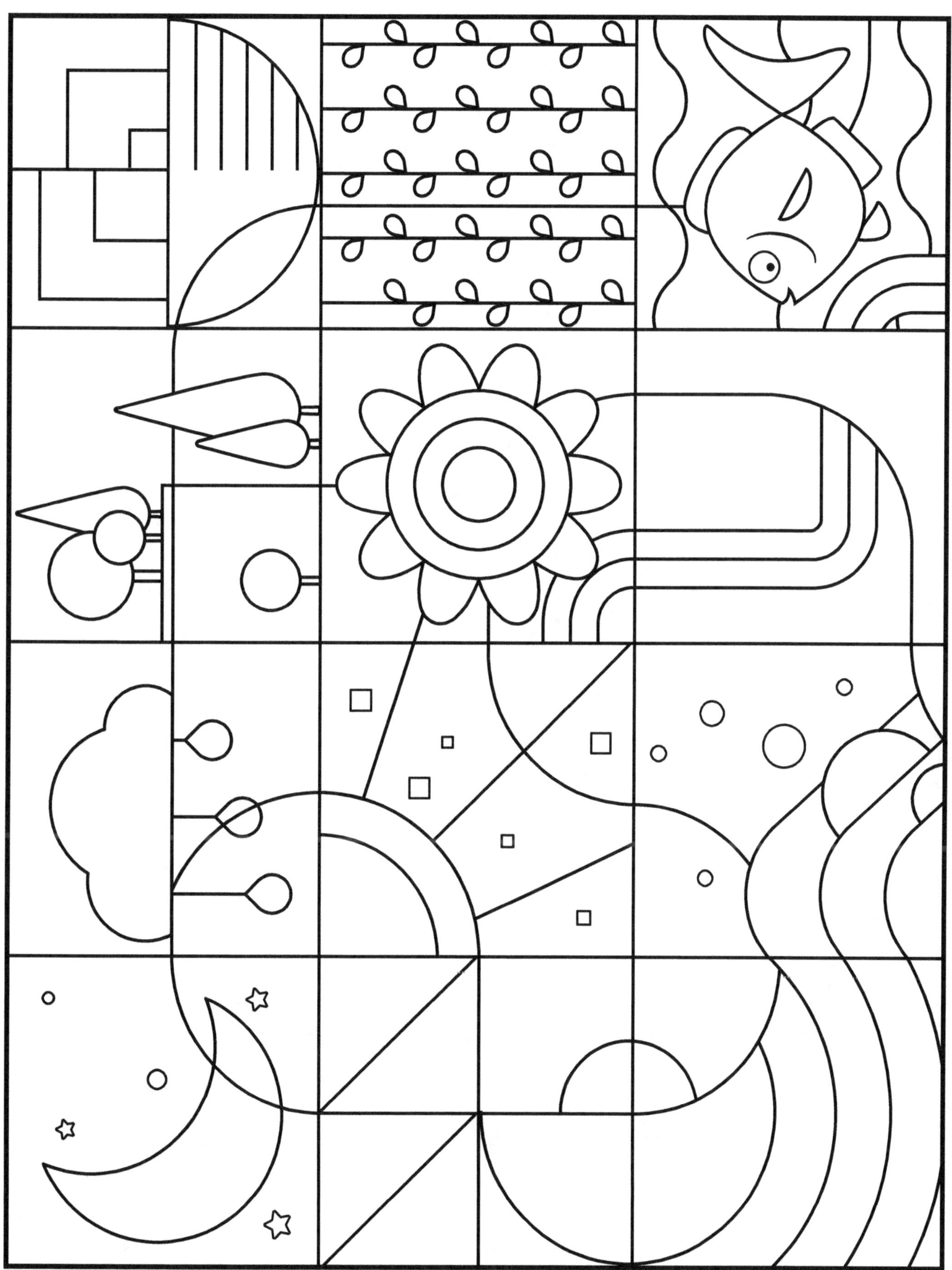

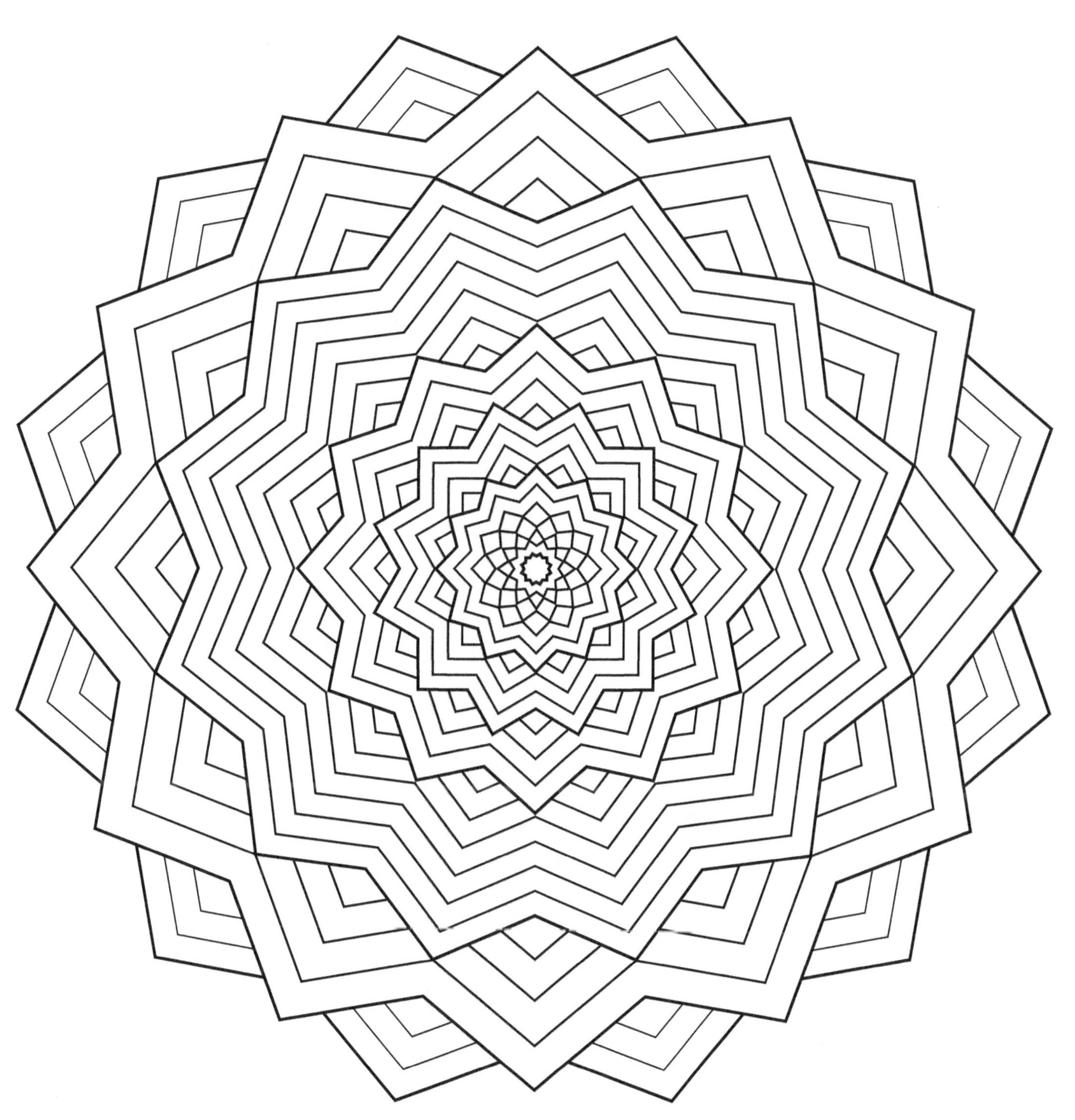

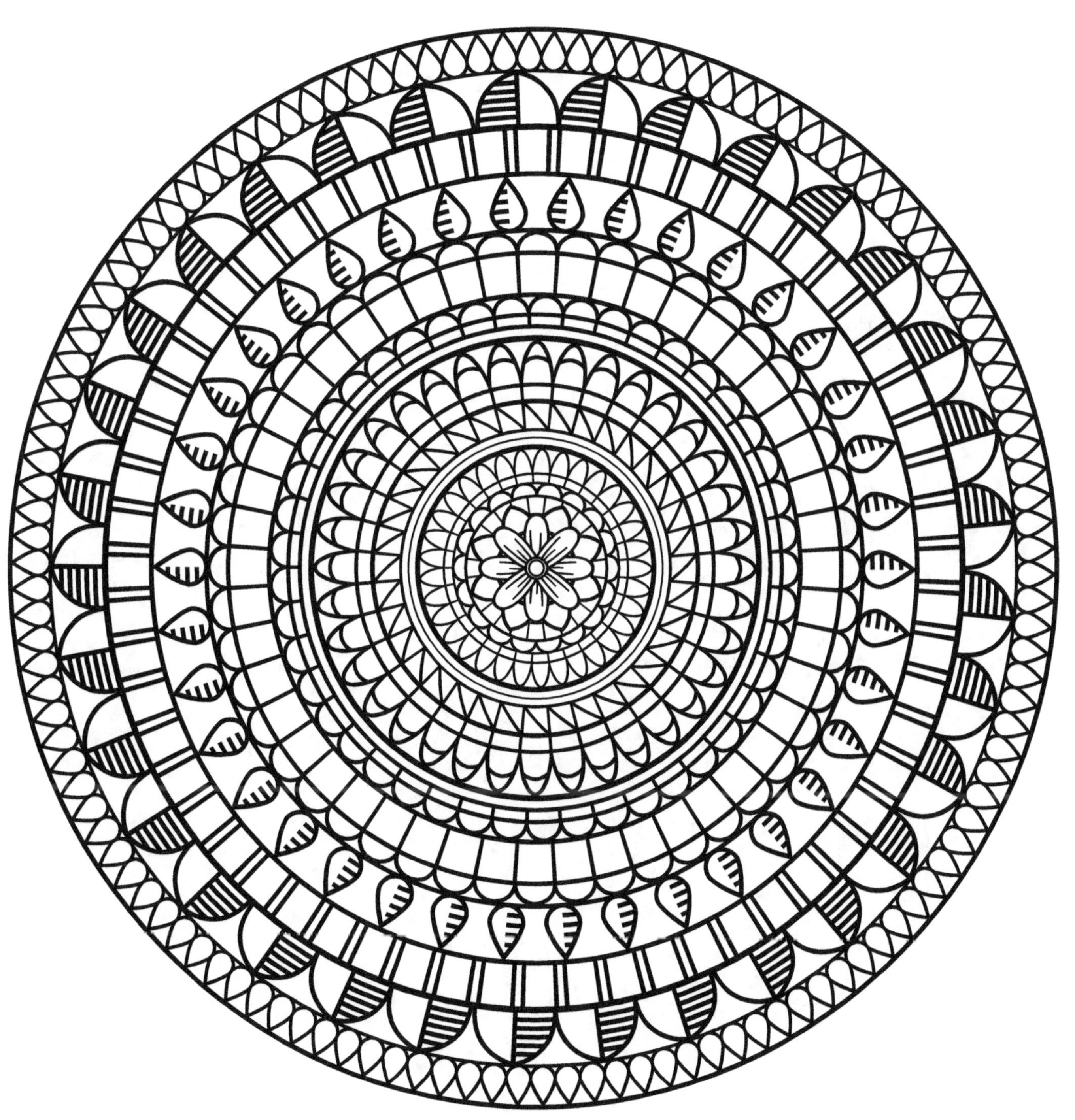

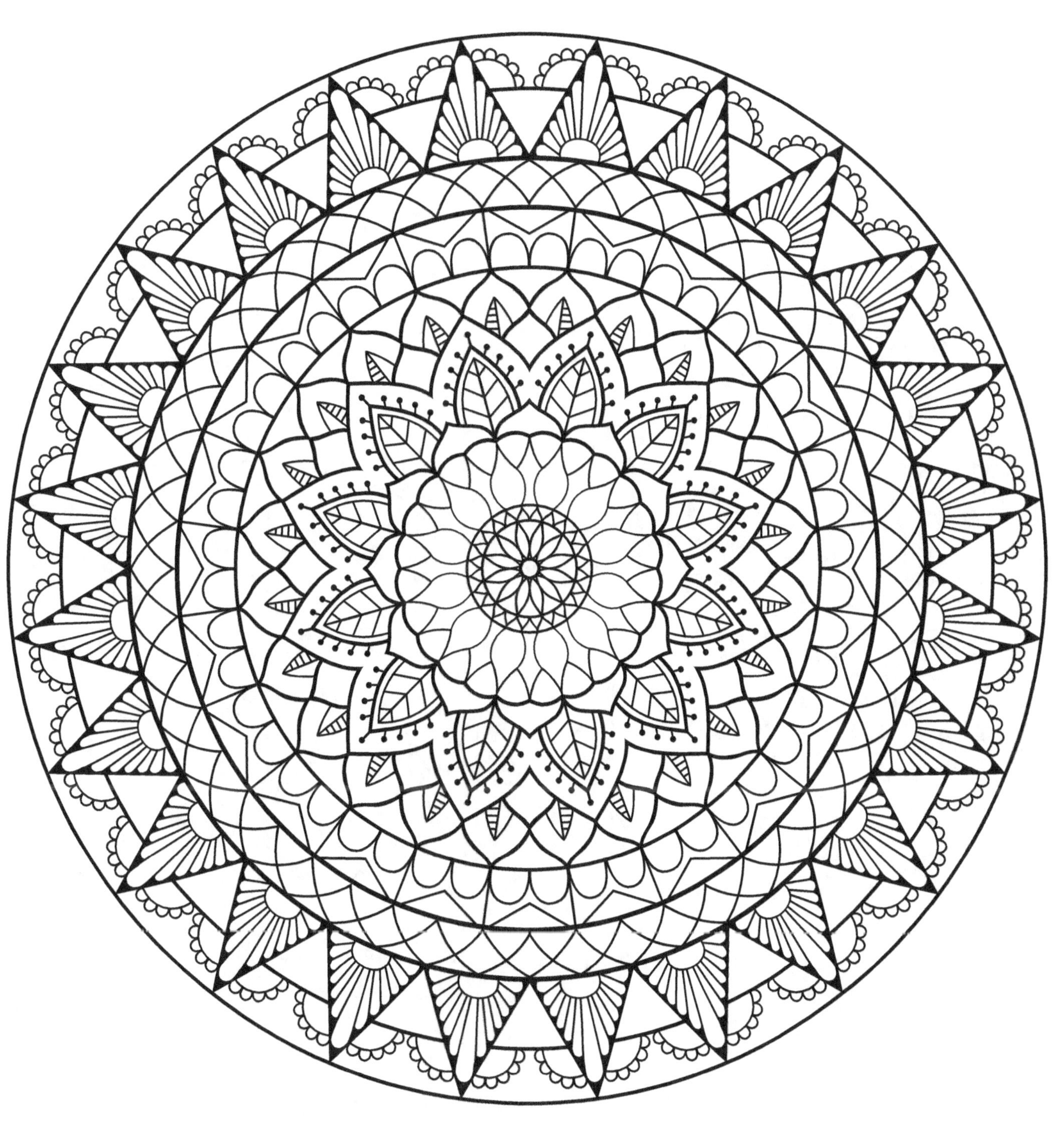

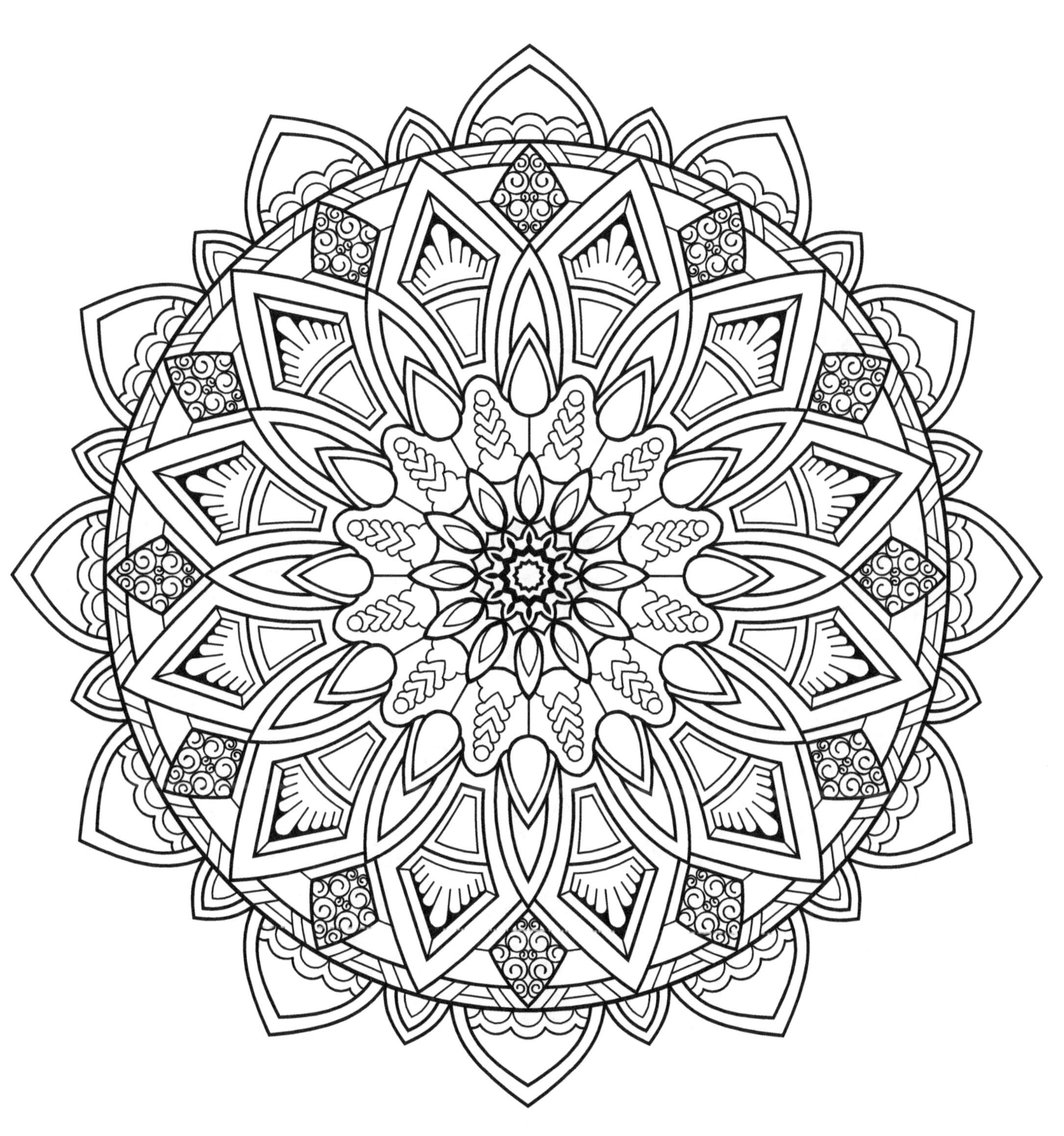

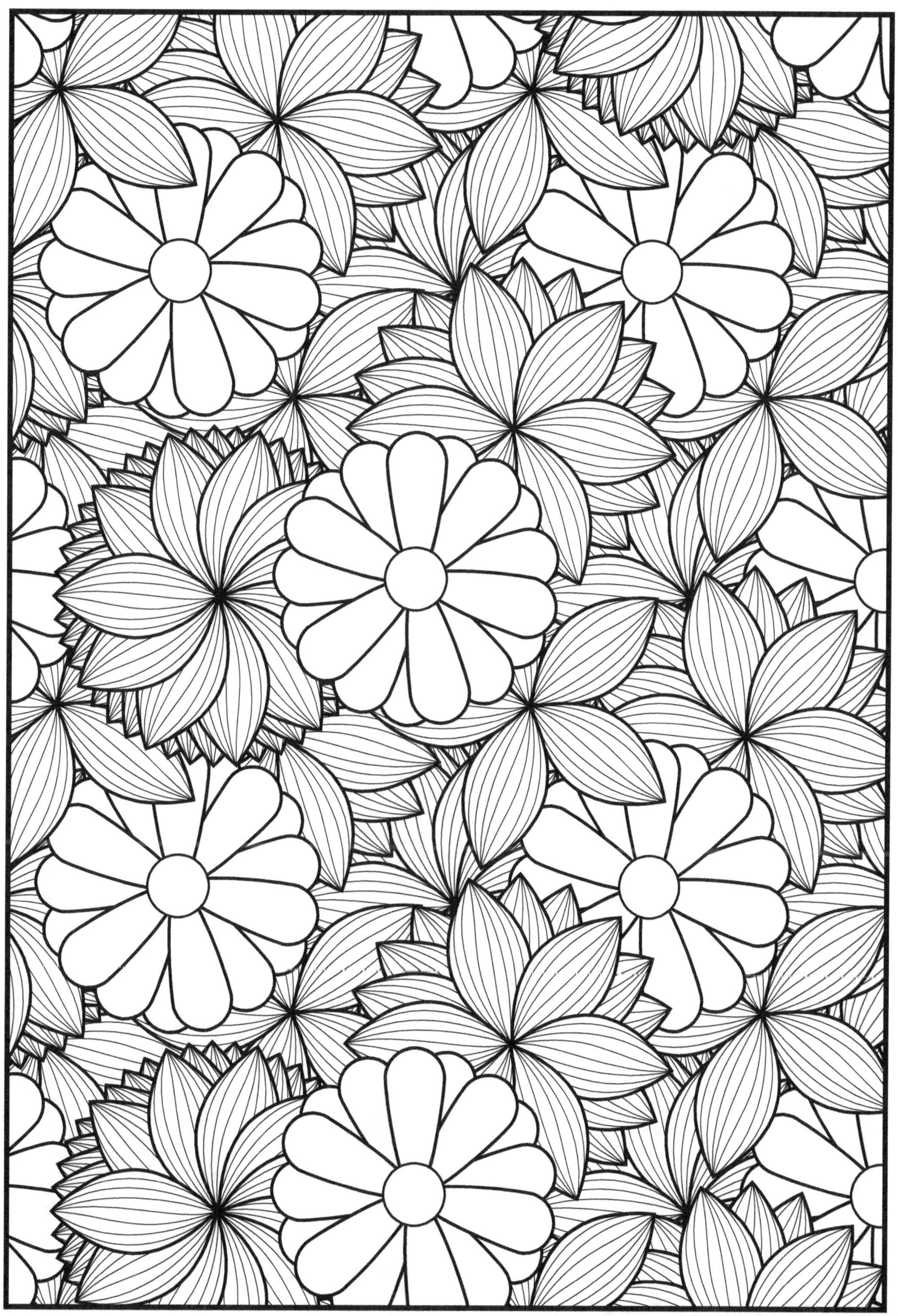

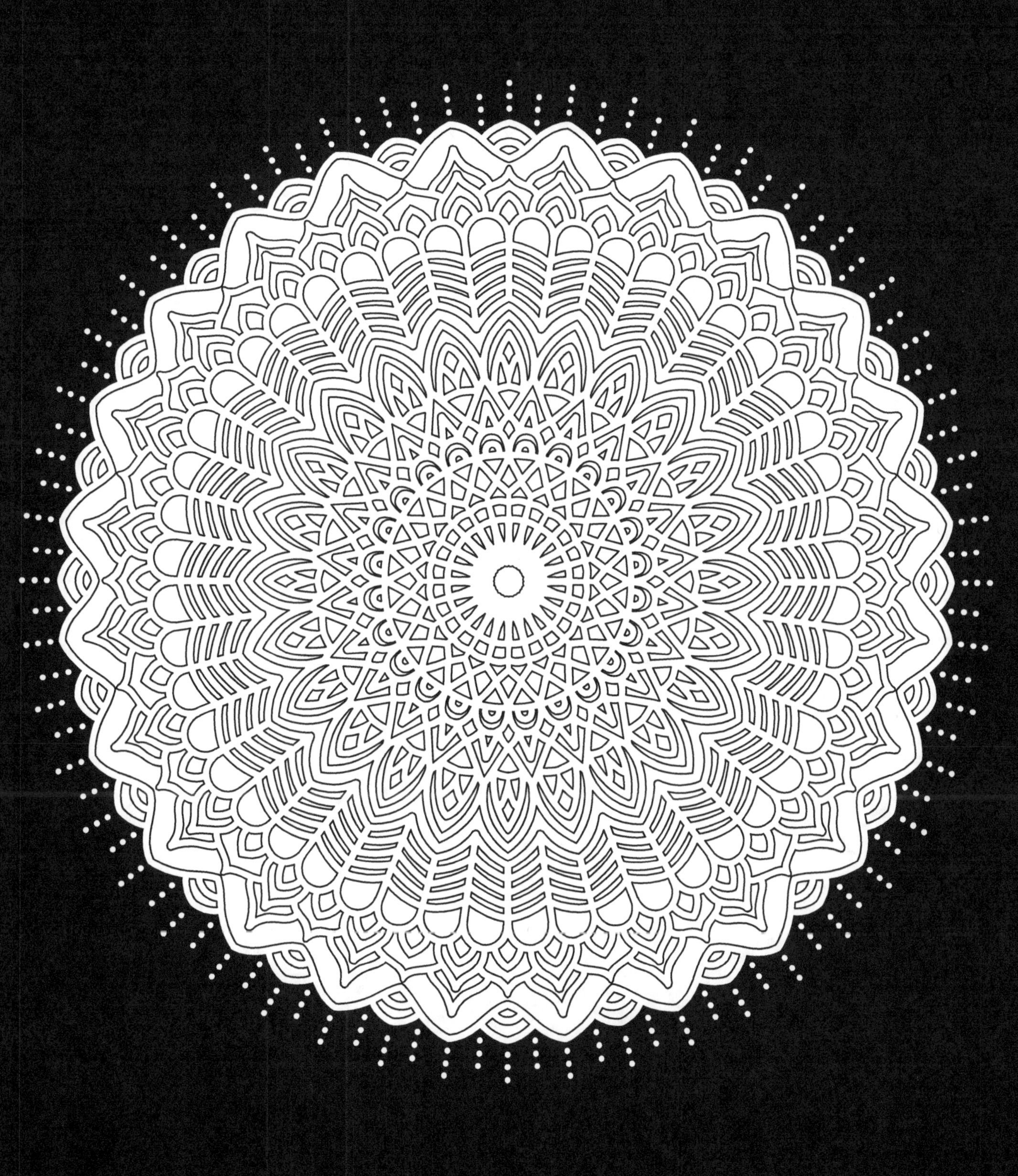

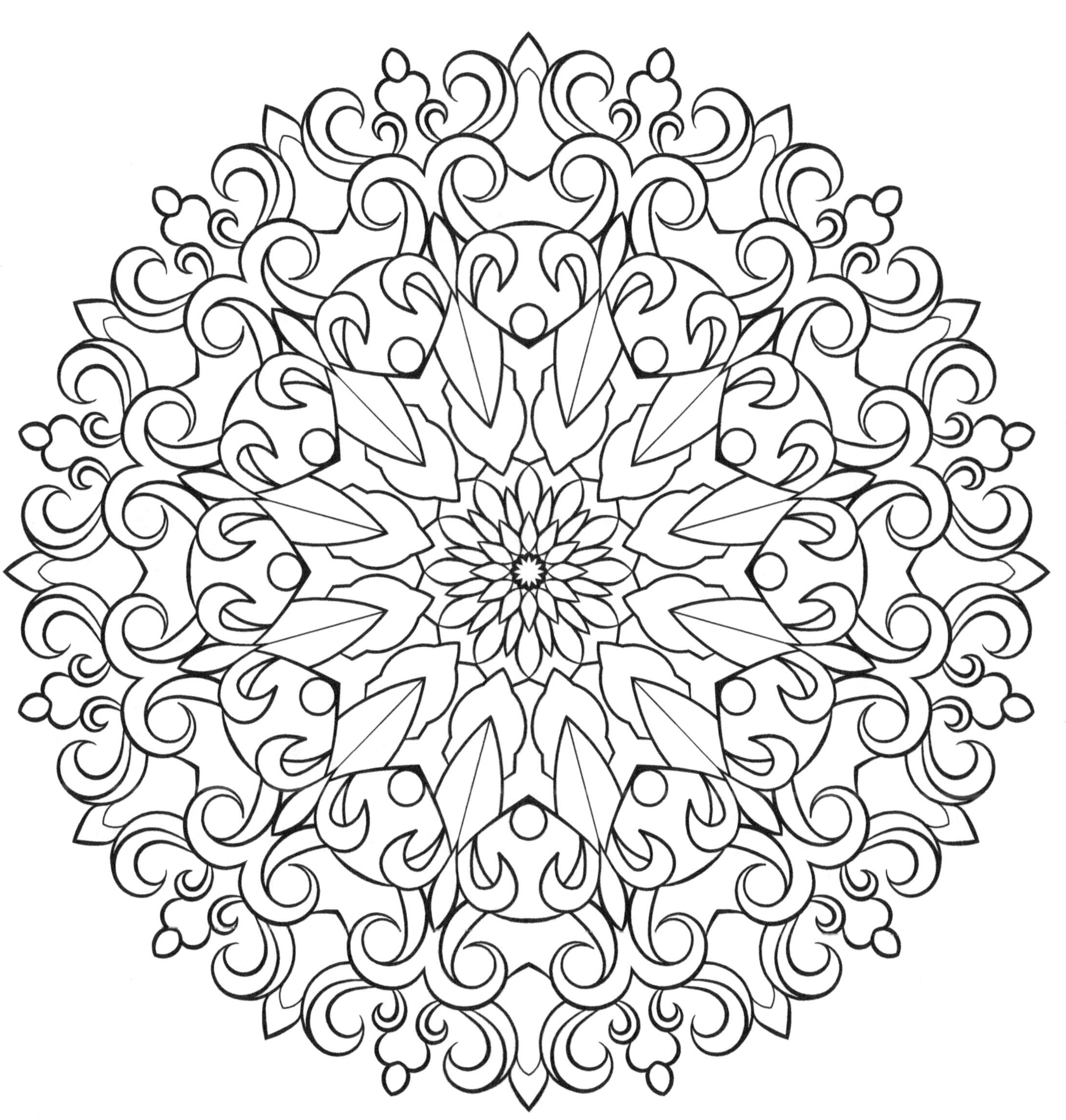

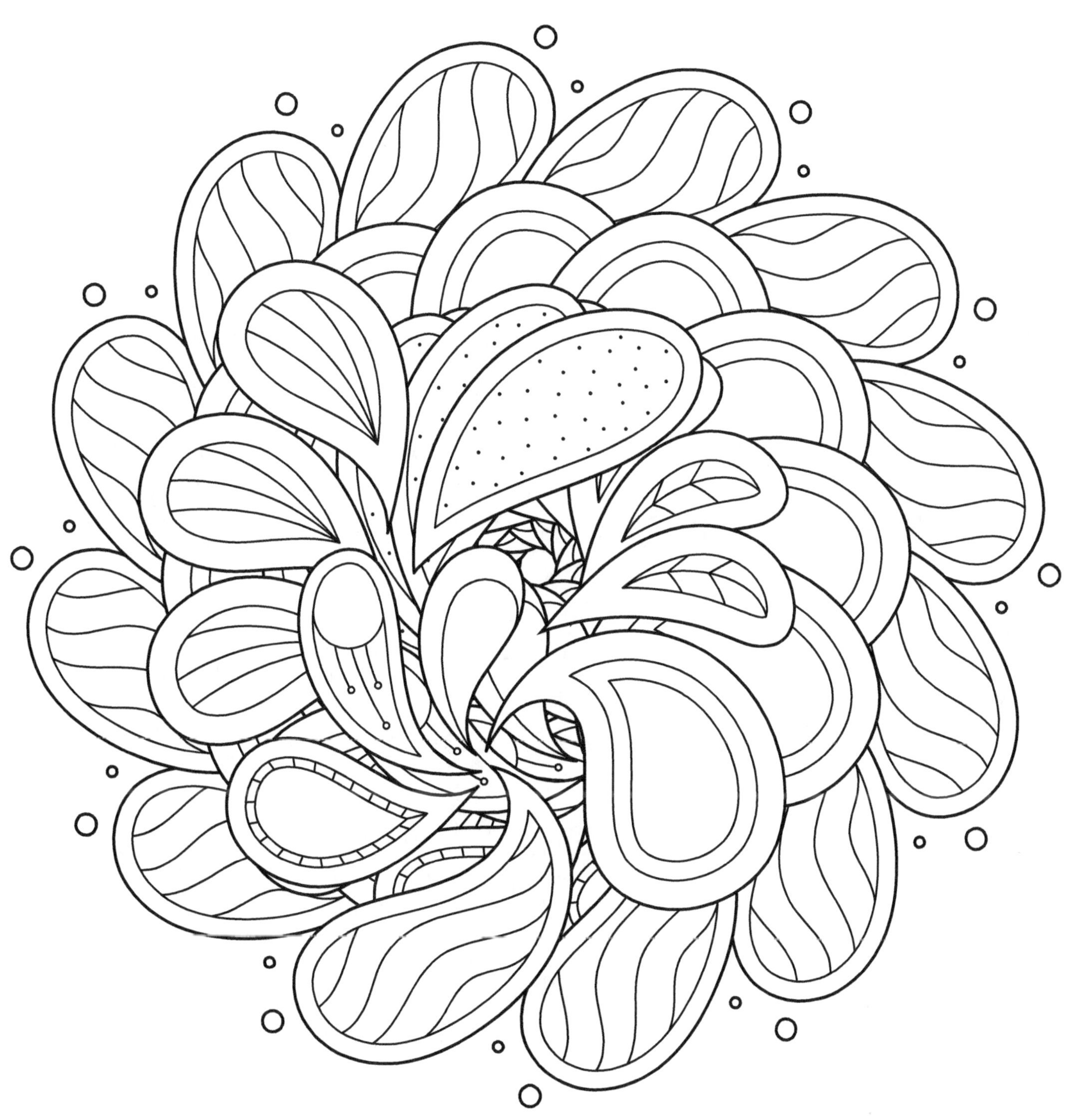

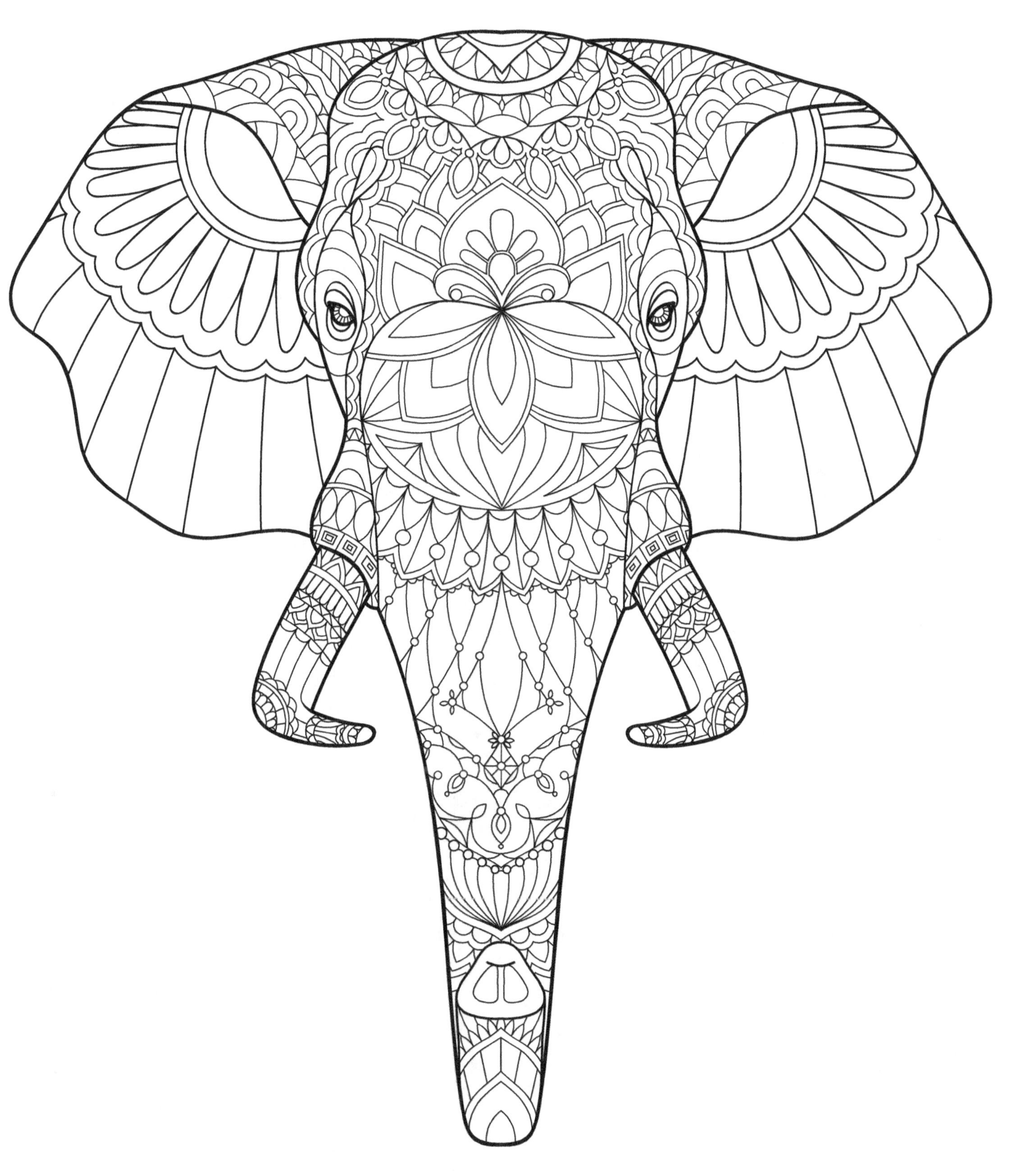

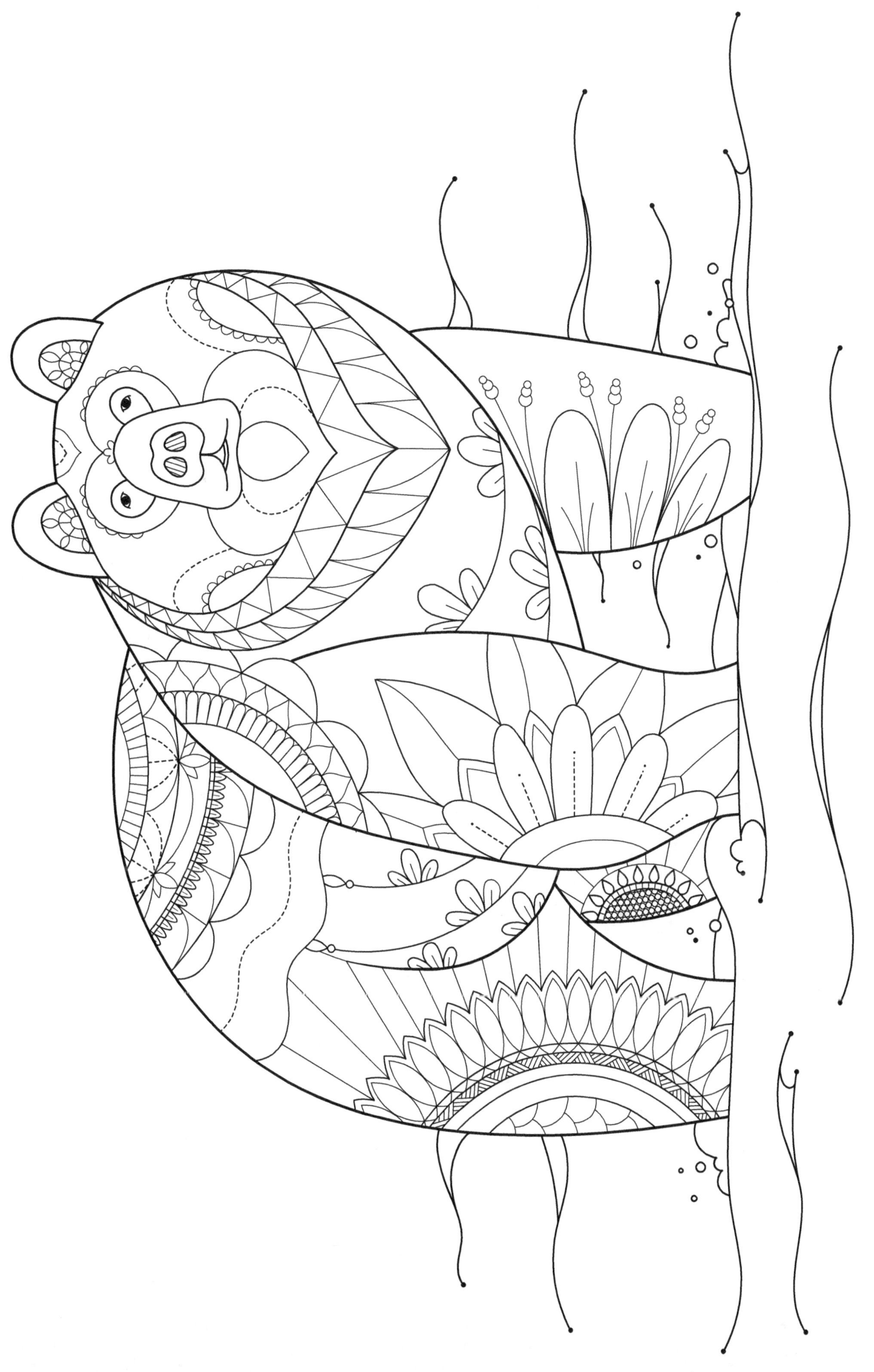

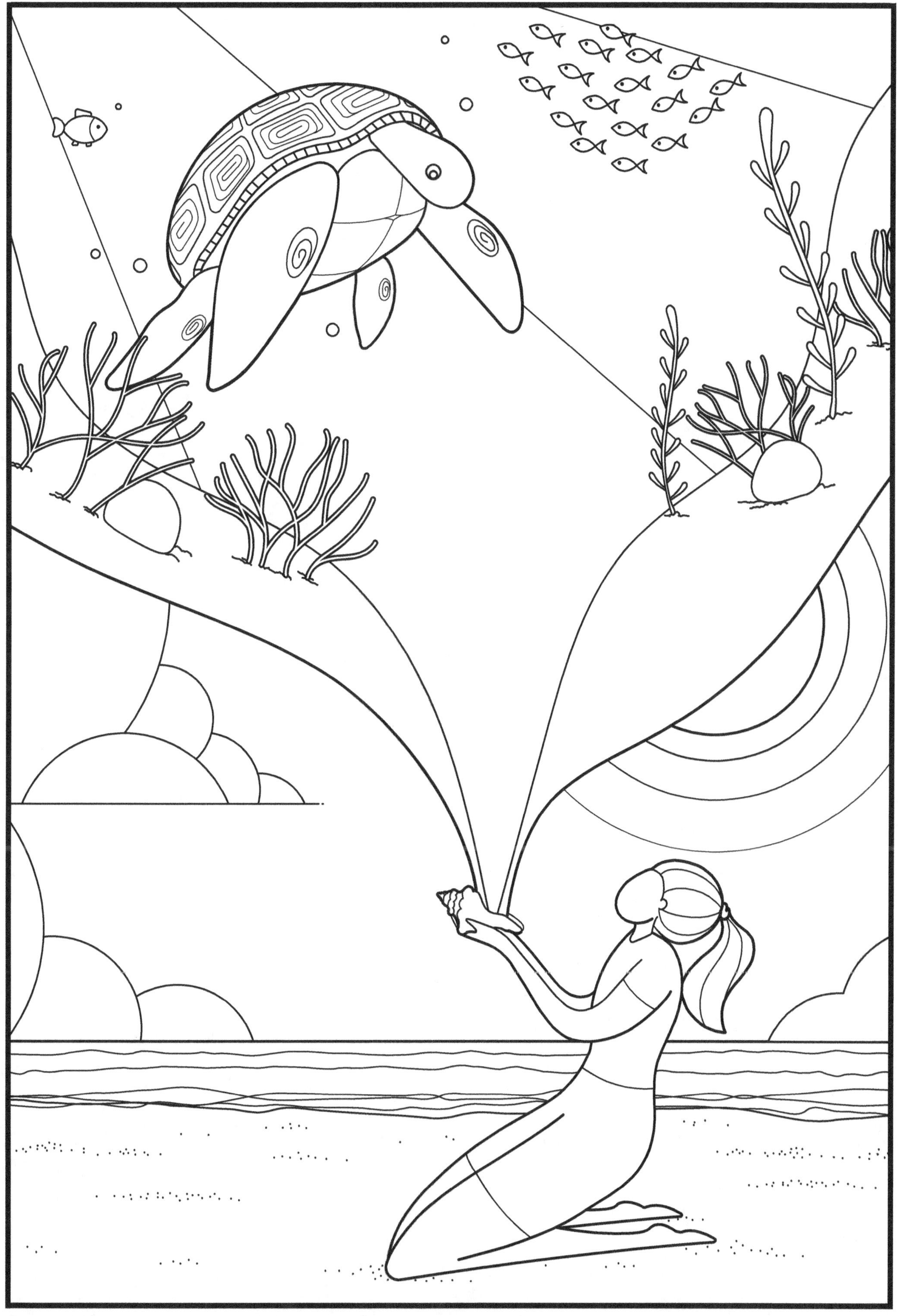

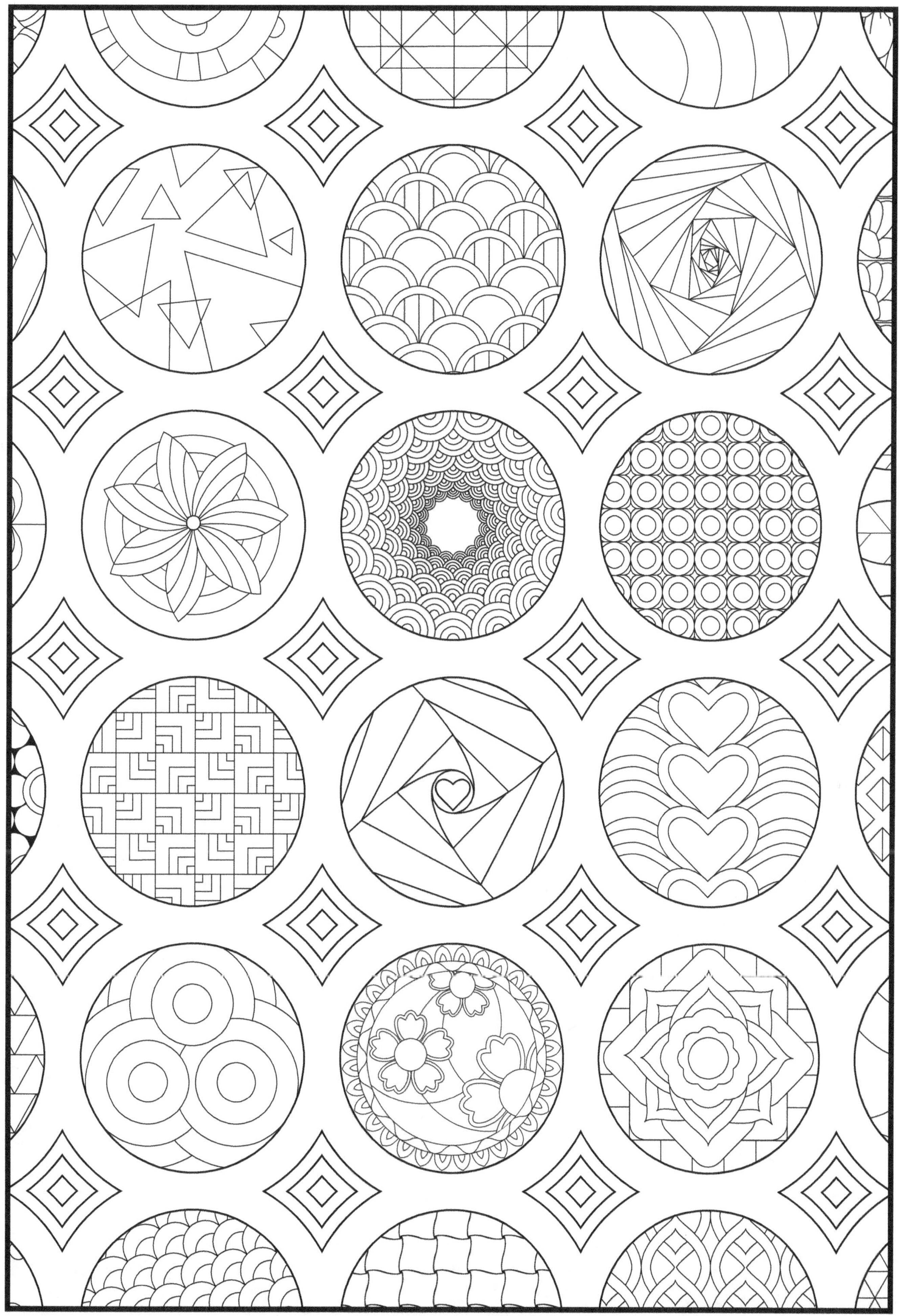

Color Palette Test Page

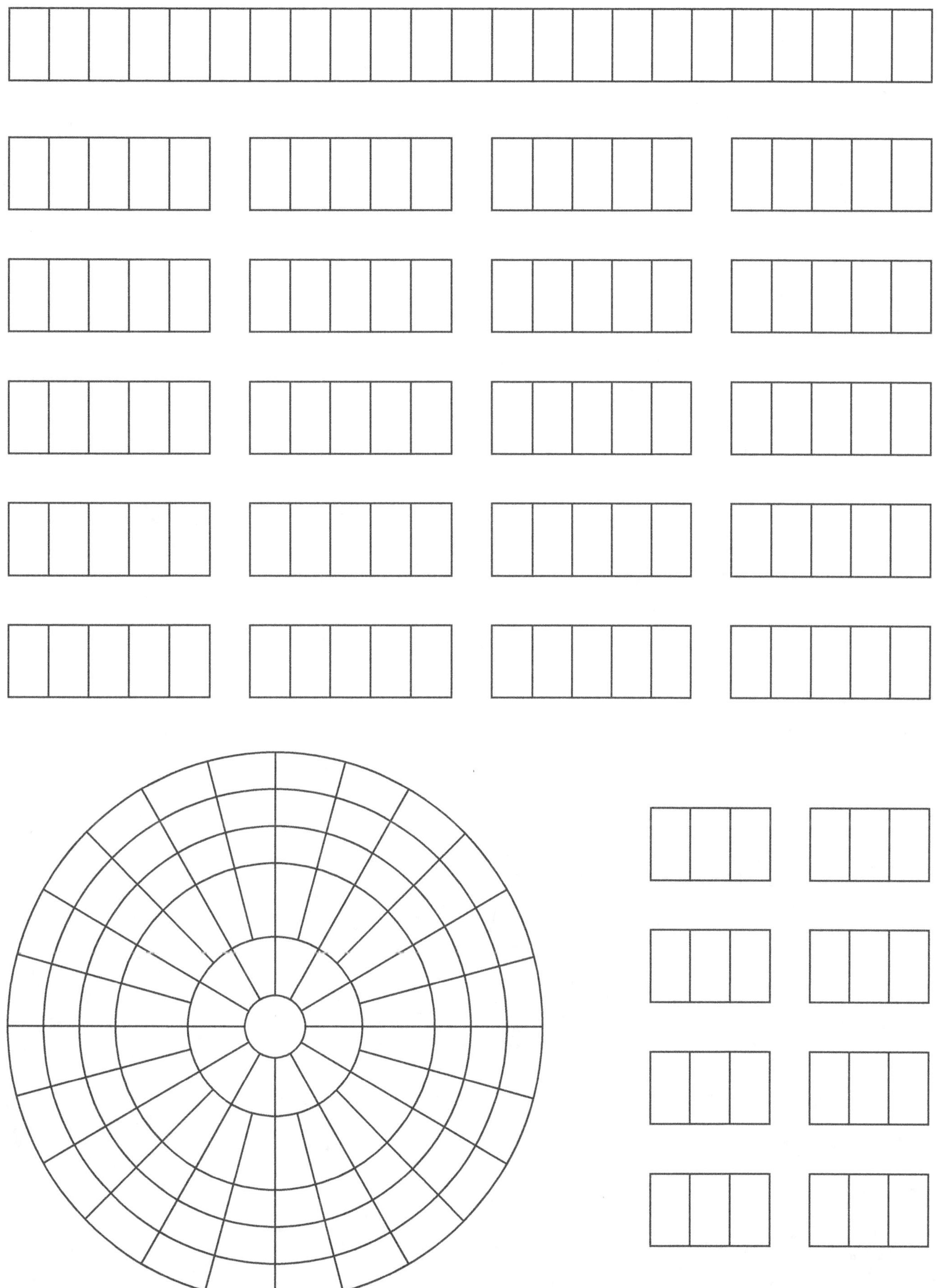